GROWING OUT OF IT

GROWING OUT OF IT

MACHINATIONS BEFORE MADNESS

LEE THOMPSON

OMNIBUS PRESS

London / New York / Paris / Sydney / Copenhagen / Berlin / Madrid / Tokyo

Dedicated to all the staff of the NHS (and emergency
services), in particular Dr Kennon and Dr Locke,
surgeons at the Royal Free Hospital, who gave me
an extension of life, and without whom, this 'can of
worms' would not have been opened!

CONTENTS

FOREWORD
Martin Freeman

I knew who Lee Thompson was before I knew his name. I'd seen him in the 'Baggy Trousers' video; he was the one flying about on wires wearing what can only be called, well, baggy trousers. He was funny but also slightly menacing, like some offshoot of the Child Catcher amongst the little football-playing kids.

'Funny and menacing' is quite a good steer for Lee's role in Madness, at least from an outsider's point of view. There was an intensity about him which meant that even when he was dressed as a regulation old granny, he was an old granny who would either nut you or implode, skanking, in a ball of flames.*

Lee's performance style is that of a natural introvert with the Tasmanian Devil busting to get out. These two things play out in constant tension, helping to drive the whole show along.

---

* *Martin refers to the videos for 'House Of Fun' and 'Our House'.*

He's a founder member of one of the best British bands ever. He's a *terrific* sax player. He's written some fine tunes. He's even a pretty good actor.

So, let's hear his story then, shall we?

INTRODUCTION
Ian 'Snowy' Snowball

It was a Saturday afternoon in February 2017 at the Museum of Comedy, just off central London's Bloomsbury Way. In the modest theatre area, I was doing an 'in conversation' event with drummer Steve White. We'd been going for about 15 minutes, with me pressing him about his time working with Paul Weller and Steve providing some amazing drumming demonstrations of tracks like 'Wild Wood'.

Suddenly, the curtain that covered the entrance flung open (after several failed attempts) and we could make out the figures of two people entering the room, in darkness, to try to find two vacant seats. Although they were doing their best to be quiet and not interrupt the event, they didn't quite pull it off.

The show must go on, so Steve and I continued. I invited the audience to ask him any questions: a few hands went up but in the back row someone stood up from the shadows. A voice introduced itself: "Hello, I'm Lee from Madness." The whole theatre turned around in one smooth motion. It turned out to be Lee Thompson with his wife, Debbie. Lee asked Steve a question about drumming and a conversation was had.

It was in the bar afterward that Lee and I got talking. From the very first, I was invited to do an 'in conversation'-style thing with him as part of the *One Man's Madness* film launch at Dingwalls in Camden. For those who haven't seen it, *One Man's Madness* is a rocku-docu-mockumentary where Lee, startlingly, takes on a number of roles. I jumped at the opportunity. As Lee and Debbie hung around to happily chat with punters and drink, we exchanged numbers and agreed to speak again soon.

The *One Man's Madness* launch came and went, and further Q&A events were added. They were all a lot of fun. Lee was easy to work with, fun to be around. His stories of growing up and the early days of Madness were captivating.

It was a few months after that I rang Lee to pitch the idea of helping him put together his autobiography, which I knew would make an excellent read. He said yes and that was the start of my Magical Madness Mystery Tour with Lee 'KIX/Thommo' Thompson, as we went through the process of writing his book.

I approached Omnibus because I considered them to be the perfect publisher and knew they'd pull out all the stops. Lee and I met with David Barraclough from Omnibus, and a contract was signed just a few weeks later.*

My only regret about working with Lee on his autobiography is that I didn't have the good fortune of

---

* Thanks for your help with this, Tony M.

knowing him for years, unlike the family and friends who contributed their insights. But I've come to know a man who is simultaneously generous, funny, humble and fascinating, someone I'd like to have hung around with.

Over the next few months, our sessions became something of an adventure. One Saturday afternoon, Lee and I agreed to meet in a service station off the M25. One thing I'd learned about him by then was that he's seldom on time. So I got to the service station early, to get some grub while I waited for him. I'd just plonked myself down into a chair and was about to tuck into my meal when my phone rang. It was Lee telling me he was in the carpark outside, in his camper van with Debbie. I stuffed some chips into my gob and went to find them. I searched the car park – but nothing.

I phoned Lee and eventually managed to track them down in the garage area. Lee apologised for the change of plan (he always did) and explained that he and Debbie were heading to see their friend, Lynn Milsom. Lee jumped into my car and we followed Debbie, who'd taken charge of the van.

A few moments later, Lee was hanging out of the window trying to get Debbie's attention. She'd taken the wrong exit and was heading down the wrong section of the M25. Eventually, I did end up drinking tea in Lynn's front room while Lee sat there in a 1960s police helmet, which he'd discovered in her home.

He and I would often meet somewhere in London. Lee might suggest a café or pub near Chancery Lane, but then he'd text or phone to ask if we could meet in, say, Camden or Highgate. I'm not overly familiar with north London so I always wondered if he did this just to keep me on my toes.

I enjoyed hearing his stories about his friends, his family, the music he'd loved, the various fashions he'd adopted, his time in approved school. I discovered there is much more to Lee Thompson than initially meets the eye, so much more to the man that so many of us saw pranking about on *Top Of The Pops* in a fez.

During one of our book sessions, I passed him a ticket for a Billy Cobham gig at Ronnie Scott's. It was for that night but something had come up and I needed to get back home to Kent. I was pleased that the ticket wasn't going to be wasted, but the following day I received a phone call from some woman at Ronnie's. She wanted payment for an unsettled drinks bill.

I was confused so I rang Lee. He told me he'd found a table and ordered some drinks, but another fella came and sat beside him who was quite annoying, so Lee decided to leave the club. He told me he'd go back to Ronnie's and settle the bill. (I don't know if he ever did. I don't know if I'm currently blacklisted from the club either...)

Lee was always inviting me to Madness gigs and I took him up on his offer several times. I went to one at the Detling Showground in Maidstone, near to where I live. Lee sorted it so that Loz, my wife, and Josie, my daughter, could also go. This was Josie's first gig and she loved it.

Lee arranged for us to see Madness again a few months later. Josie and I travelled with him and his son, Daley, to the venue in Thetford Forest, East Anglia. It was a hot, sunny Saturday during the 2018 World Cup and England were playing. Two hours before Lee was due to perform in front of five thousand people, we were stood in a country beer garden watching the first half of the game. During halftime we jumped back in our cars and raced off to the venue, where we watched the second half of the game backstage with other members of Madness and the crew.

Josie and I watched Madness play their gig whilst dancing at the side of the stage. Wow! What a view! What an experience! It was a special day that my daughter and I will never forget. Thank you Lee, thank you Madness – you made us feel very welcome.

Throughout 2018 and into 2019, Lee and I knuckled down. A part of me didn't want the process to end. We'd started off with the intention of writing a chronological autobiography, from the cradle to the grave (well, *not quite…*), but soon realised such a book would probably end up longer than *War And Peace* or a Genesis album. So we decided to only go up to the release of 'One Step Beyond…' – we'd set our goal, but en route (as with many of my meetings with Lee) the destination changed. We refined our idea, settling on the book only going up to the release of 'The Prince' – which seemed fitting, as 2019 was the 40-year anniversary of that song.

Lee tells the story of his life growing up in London NW5. He shares experiences of his schooling and the scrapes he often got into, which brought him into regular contact with the law. But amidst all of this, Lee discovered fashion: skinheads and suedeheads were the movement of the day, and he connected to the look of Ben Sherman shirts, Sta-Prest trousers and highly polished brogues. And then there was the music: Lee fell in love with ska and reggae, which would lend itself to what he'd go on to write in Madness; then there was glam rock, the pub-rock explosion on his north London doorstep, and punk – the huge influence that decided him to take up the saxophone and form the band that would, by 1978, become Madness.

Lee describes what it was like in the early days of Madness: the rehearsals, the sackings, the song-writing process, the gigs, the first recording sessions, and being included on the legendary 2Tone Tour. His memoir is full of humour, character, friendship, hardship and crime. It's also a history lesson on the fashions and musical genres of the 1970s. It really is a mad story!

1

NW5

Performing with Madness on the roof of Buckingham Palace for the Queen's Diamond Jubilee. Being part of the Olympics Closing Ceremony in that same year – 2012. Creating earthquakes in Finsbury Park. Fifteen top-ten singles and a respectable list of successful albums. Still being in the game after forty years, with a bunch of mates I consider to be amongst my closest friends. None of this would have been possible without my mum – on account of I'd never have been born...

Mum was born Lillian Scannell in 1925, one of four children including my Uncle Jack, Auntie Eileen, who was wheelchair-bound since an ill-fated operation in the 1930s, and Uncle Pat. Mum was the second youngest. Their own mother had passed on in 1948 when they were still quite young adults. Her name was Florence, which was also my mum's middle name.

Mum was a Londoner born and bred, growing up in Eversholt Street, which is a long road between Euston and

King's Cross train stations. It was a busy, working-class area of the city. Some old Victorian flats served as the family home, and it was from that building that she observed a recovering London shaking off the shadows of the Great War.

Mum was very much the matriarch of our family – she had to be, due to my dad's lifestyle. She was extremely clean and tidy, something which has rubbed off on me. If you were smoking a fag in the front room and using the ashtray, it would be removed, cleaned out and returned before you finished your smoke. Shoes off, wash your hands, toilet seat up, turn lights off after you!

Mum had an incredible amount of energy, always on the go and flitting from one thing to the next. She never seemed to stop and relax. Mum was also very concerned about me and my future, keeping a close eye on how I invested my time and my money, once Madness started to become successful. Her generation's attitude towards money was very careful and that's rubbed off on me too. Like Ronnie Barker's character Arkwright said: "Nobody got rich by spending."

Whenever I acquired any money, filthy lucre or not, I always made sure Mum was looked after. Being as I was her only son, the sun really did shine out of my backside, and whenever she had a few extra bob she'd spoil me rotten.

My dad was Fredrick Thompson and he was born in Great Yarmouth, Norfolk, one of thirteen children. His dad died when I was about six years old and I have a photograph of me standing beside his grave. From what I can gather, he was a man who certainly enjoyed his life – a character among characters. My dad worked in the market at Great

Yarmouth, as did my grandfather, Charles. People who knew him said my grandad was a song-and-dance man at the market after a pub lunch!

During the war, my mum had a stint living in Kent before working in Great Yarmouth. It was in the late 1940s that she found employment waitressing in one of Britain's most popular seaside towns, and it was also there that my mum and dad met and started their relationship. But London had a huge attraction for my dad, with much more to offer him than Great Yarmouth.

My parents got married in 1953, the year of the Queen's coronation, settling in north London at 12 Denyer House on the Highgate Road. That's where my mum and dad were living when I came along. My mum gave birth to me in the University College Hospital on Warren Street.

My earliest memories are rooted in Denyer House. It wasn't just my parents and me who lived there. There was also my granddad, my cousin Vince and his mum, Auntie Eileen, and nearby were Uncle Jack and Uncle Pat. So I had a lot of family surrounding me, as did a lot of people back then. It wasn't unusual to have several family members living within bowling distance.

My granddad seemed to walk everywhere. His mode of transport was a pushbike, as he detested motorcars, which he saw as smoky, noisy, dangerous contraptions. To get me out the house, he'd take me on Sunday morning walks over Waterlow Park, Kite Hill, Regent's Park and Primrose Hill, down Kentish Town Road, through Camden Town, stopping at Somers Town in time for 'early doors'. Well, 12 noon until 2pm... 2.45pm if the guvnor was in a good mood. Those were the rules. Restricted times were still in place, brought into effect due to the war effort. Grandad would meet some old mates, who were lucky enough to get through both world wars. I always felt this was his favourite time of the week: showing me off, sinking a few jars, having a joke, a few belly laughs. He'd then get us both home for Mum's Sunday dinner, which was cabbage juice with pepper! Dessert? Fruit jelly and tinned Carnation milk – yuk! After dinner, he'd take a 'Churchill nap' before sloping over to the Southampton Arms at 7pm, for a few more 'chemical coshes'. I have many good memories of him. He was good, kind and very hard working. I admired his working-class attitude. He was the best. Same as my father-in-law, John.

*   *   *

I was born on October 5, 1957. Paul Anka was king of the charts with his latest single, 'Diana', Pat Boone and Harry Belafonte were hot on his heels – and of course, the real King of Rock'n'Roll, Elvis, was roaring up the charts with Leiber and Stoller's blistering 'Jailhouse Rock'.

The daily rags wrote about Stirling Moss tearing up the Grand Prix; Harold Macmillan was the new Tory Prime Minister and continued to fly the blue flag high and mighty; *The Bridge On The River Kwai* was a cinema smash; the Wolfenden Report was bold enough to recommend homosexuality between consenting adults 'in private' should no longer be a criminal offence.

It wasn't much more than a decade after the Second World War and things were getting shaken up, attitudes were being tested. The next decade was going to take Britain on a whole new Magical Mystery Tour, and I had a ticket for that journey.

The likes of Sid Vicious, Siouxsie Sioux, Billy Bragg, Danny Baker and Dawn French also bowed into the world in 1957, and entertainers from the old world, such as Scot comic Harry Gordon and ventriloquist Fred Russell, bowed out. It was a gradual process but Britain was clawing itself away from the post-war black-and-white landscape, where sons dressed like their dads, who also dressed like their own dads, in dull and drab woollen tank tops. Colour was being introduced and a teenager could just about get away with wearing a pink shirt, as he strolled down Camden High Street humming a Billy Fury song.

Of course, I was far too young to witness the rock'n'roll of the 1950s, with the teddy boys' quiffs, crepes and Edwardian drapes, and girls in stiletto heels and dresses within dresses (with petticoats underneath, like the later ra-ra skirts of the 1980s). I'd be aware enough of what was going on in the 1960s, but I don't recall seeing groups or gangs hanging around my area. More likely they were at the Lyceum or Hammersmith Palais; Soho and west London would be magnets for the after-hours thrill seekers.

My sister Tracy was born in January 1961. I don't have any early memories of her arriving into the family, just of us dancing together in the bedroom when she was a little bit older. She tripped and banged her head on a bit of furniture, and my mum came in and screamed at us. She certainly got our attention!

Tracy and I have always got on well. Growing up, we had a lot of the same interests. I think I played the role of her bigger brother well. She idolised me and I looked after her as my only sister. Even today, we still talk with one another on a regular basis.

Tracy adored our dad, too, and was very much the daddy's girl. He could do no wrong in her eyes. There was a time, when we were living in Luton, when Tracy and my mum didn't get along, but they got over that once we moved back to London.

My mum was very protective about Tracy and me in Luton. I think Tracy had started to knock about with some lads, who my mum sniffed out pretty quickly as being unsavoury. Tracy could be a rebel too, especially during the periods when my dad wasn't around. She pushed the boundaries and thought she could do as she pleased.

Tracy Thompson: Our dad was a bit hooky and Lee was a bit like that when he was growing up. We all thought Lee was going to take after him. But he didn't and that surprised some of us. If anything, he went in a completely different direction. I don't believe getting into the band made a difference, I just think Lee was always going to do his own thing. He has a different personality to our mum and dad. Lee is quite placid, but our mum and me could get very irate. We had tempers. That's not Lee.

My dad had various jobs when I was growing up. Some were actually legitimate too. For a period of time he was a minicab driver and on some occasions he'd actually take me along with him. He told me I was his security guard, which made me feel special and needed. We'd drive all over

London and every now and then he'd would pull the car over and disappear into some house for a few minutes. In truth, I have no idea what he was up to but I'm confident it wasn't anything drug-related. He detested anything to do with drug-taking.

Other than that, my dad's career was as a thief. He'd rob warehouses and freight lorries for a 'parcel of goods'. Rumour has it that my dad's and one other gang were the only ones to use dynamite in their exploits. This meant that whenever dynamite was used in any robbery, the police always came looking for him first.

I was a small boy when I realised what my dad's 'job' was. I can especially remember one Christmas because, when I came down to the living room early in the morning, the Christmas tree was surrounded with presents. There were also bottles of Scotch and stacks of cigarettes, but they were still in their Benson & Hedges boxes so that pretty much gave it away.

As a consequence of my dad's career, he spent more time away in prison than he did with my mum, my sister and me. This was something that we, as a family, had to learn to accept. By the time I was a young man, I discovered that my dad had a criminal history dating back to when he was eighteen.*

Having Tracy and me didn't deter my dad from his chosen path. We were simply told what to say if nosey Parkers asked about him: Dad was 'away, working abroad'. We had some

---

* Prior to this age, the authorities were supposed to destroy the individual's criminal record.

relatives that worked on the oil rigs, so sometimes we told people that Dad was up north drilling and would be away for several months. Of course, Tracy and I knew the truth: he was sitting in some cold cell next to a bucket of piss, probably plotting his next robbery.

By the time I understood why Dad was away, I didn't feel angry with him. If anything, I just hoped he'd get away with it because I wanted him to be at home with Mum, Tracy and me. Mum took me to see him in prison lots of times. I remember going to HMP Parkhurst on the Isle of Wight, which was like a day trip out for me: I think we had to get a train, a bus, a boat, another train and then another bus. But at the end of it, I got to see my old man and I'd hang onto every word he said.

When I did see him, he reminded me of Dracula as he was pale due to not getting any sunlight. In the summer months, if I saw somebody who had milky skin, I'd naively assume they'd just got out from a two-year stretch. My dad was in many different prisons and after a while they just looked the same to me – tall brick walls and windows with bars on them. The visits I used to look forward to turned rather daunting.

My mum was actually very embarrassed about my dad's 'work'. It was very much a case of 'Oh dear, what will the neighbours think?' In truth, they had all probably worked it out for themselves. People knew each other's business back in those days. Unlike nowadays, people actually knew who their neighbours were and would gossip and find stuff out about so-and-so.

Maybe it's a reaction against my mum's response, but I'm the complete opposite. I don't really give two fucks what people think about me. I've seen a lot of it during my time in the music business – a lot of people get very hurt because of other people's judgments. It can be very cruel and have long-lasting effects.

So I'm very much a two-fingers-up type of person when it comes to what other people think of me. I couldn't be the person that I've been in Madness if I was any other way. That probably goes for Suggs, too. The band were never much good at praising each other, only polishing each other's egos or giving it that brotherly touch if need be.

As I got older, I realised I wasn't going to be the type of person to just sit back with cap in hand, waiting for someone to toss in a few pennies. Instead, my dad's influence grew on me and I started to go down a similar path to him.

One of my dad's favourite interests was gambling. He was a punter. I've known him to put two grand down on a horse back in the early 1970s, a lot of money back then. Walthamstow Dogs was always an eventful and eye-opening evening out, it showed me how adults had fun!

At Walthamstow race meetings, there were many loud and emotional punters screaming at a bunch of greyhounds chasing a stuffed rabbit. When the race had finished and the dipped floodlights came back up, they'd either be jumping with joy or cursing and cunting everything in sight.

I decided at an early age that, with gambling, no one is a winner. So I resolved never to bet on anything – well, apart from the odd one-armed bandit at the arcade.

Gambling is all about the thrill, I suppose. The family always knew when Dad had a win or a loss, because you'd either get a bag of chips or be treated to a fillet steak. He was a punter up to the point of addiction, so he could take a gamble or leave it depending on how flush he was. Mum was the compulsive one, so she was constantly at it, studying the sports section in the daily rag, picking out the trainer, jockey and, quirkily, the name of the horse: Fast Freddie, Lassie Get Home, Mr Lee…

I can remember many occasions when I'd be crouched down beside the TV, with my hand covering the horses she hadn't betted on. I would be trying to weave some magic and drag the other horses back, so that it'd be my mum's horse that won the race. I did like the way she screamed with delight when her horse won, that's a sound that will always stay with me. And of course, what we had for tea depended on whether she'd won or lost.

Despite both my parents being gamblers, I didn't inherit their passion at all. In fact, I'm the complete opposite and this, I believe, is because of my parents. Gambling is poison to me and I have no fond memories of slipping into betting offices as a kid, entering a heavily packed, smoke-filled room with the moans and groans and occasional yelps of the punters. It made me feel uncomfortable and sickened. I seemed to spend many hours waiting around betting offices, smoke rubbing away at my eyelids, all just for a bag of chips.

Dad would also be involved with hard-core card sessions in the local pubs, where he wouldn't leave the table until he'd won it all or lost it all. Although he was a quiet, laidback man, when he did blow a fuse you knew about it – especially in my early teenage years.

When Mum set a time of 10pm, you would stick to it or suffer the consequences. Which was difficult, as I was with a mixed bunch of streetwise, fun-loving mates. We could wind each other up and I was normally the one that stormed off to avoid any confrontation – I hated it. But, being as I was little and lovable, tall Dave Nash or gorgeous Tina with the cat's eyes would calm me down and bring me back into the circle. Mum would nag Dad relentlessly though, to the point of me taking a clump. If it was on my backside I'd lose control of the waterworks – though this was rare.

> **Tracy:** Dad was away in prison quite a lot, so mum had to do her best. She never had much money but she manged to keep a really good home for us. I'm sure she borrowed money from time to time, because Lee and me never went without. If we wanted something, she'd do her best to get it.

As a family we were always struggling financially, but not dire or threadbare – just a little pinched. With Dad being away so much it fell on my mum to provide for Tracy and me. I've had my fair share of living on bread and beef dripping, or sugar sandwiches. In fact I actually miss it now, but can you imagine pouring a load of sugar in between two doorstop slices of bread and getting stuck into that? It's outrageous now to think that's what we used to have for tea once or twice a week.

Then there was 'Uncle Ted', the black-cab driver who'd come round the house on the odd occasion, stinking of Brylcreem and very moody. He'd often treat me and my mum but I was wary of him hanging around, stinking the place out.

My mum worked several jobs when I was a kid. One was in a minicab office right next door to the betting office, where she (conveniently) also put in a few hours, on the Highgate Road smack-bang next to the Southampton Arms pub, my grandad's local. When I went to see her, she'd pass half a crown over the counter and tell me to go over to buy some fish and chips.

Mum also worked as a cleaner and I'd sometimes have to go along with her, if schools were out. She did the cleaning in some of the big houses in the Highgate and Kentish Town area, where we lived. Everything was in walking distance so I'd help out by carrying things for her.

I was fortunate to have made lots of friends as a kid. From the days of my first school at Gospel Oak on Mansfield Road, I always connected with someone. There was a boy called Tony Hilton who I used sit next to, we're still mates to this day. We ended up going in separate directions and then, a few years later, we found ourselves sitting beside each other again at the Acland Burghley Comprehensive School in Tufnell Park. Tony was particularly good at art and I was capable, so we'd sit in class and draw caricatures of the teachers.

Tony Hilton: Both Lee and I started at Gospel Oak Primary school at the age of about five or six, around 1963, and were in the same class. My earliest memory of this period is when he and I were both thrown out of the classroom for misbehaving by our teacher, Miss Mills. We then decided to pilfer from the cloakroom. I can still vividly remember the proceeds of this crime being a toy plastic clock, a threepenny bit and a packet of potato crisps. How sad is that? But it was the writing on the wall.

My first teacher at Gospel Oak Primary School was called Miss Mills. I got on well with her, even though I was probably the most disruptive pupil in the class. She really did try to help me because I was a bit slower than the other kids. I was still plodding my way through book one when the rest of the class were racing their way through book three.

I wasn't great at reading. I struggled with it and couldn't quite string all the words together. I remember feeling very awkward about that. But Miss Mills paid me the attention that I needed and she helped me to progress. I can't say I experienced that with all my teachers. Other than art, English grammar was my favourite lesson.

Paul Catlin: I know Lee from back in primary-school days and he was a naughty kid even then, but I actually met him just before he came to my school. I was standing on one side of Chetwynd Road in NW5 with a couple of other kids and Lee was on the other. We were in quite a rundown area, with packs of dogs running around, overgrown thistles and derelict old buildings. I could see that Lee was holding a kitten so I shouted out, "What you doing?" I could see that he wasn't hurting it or anything like that, I was just curious. But I did tell him to leave the kitten alone. He told me he wouldn't because he wasn't doing anything wrong.

He realised I was about to charge across the road, so he put the kitten down and tore off. I chased him, thinking to myself I was going to catch the naughty little fucker. I did and that business got dealt with. The next thing I know he's turned up at my school, which was Brookfield Primary. I think he'd been expelled from his own. During break time I noticed him being bullied by this other kid. I didn't like bullies so I intervened and sorted it out. The next thing, we're sitting beside each other in the classroom, drawing, and now we're mates.

If Lee could get away with something he would. He'd do stuff like trace an image and then claim he'd drawn it by hand. I'm not sure the teachers ever believed him but he had charm and he was funny, so he did kind of get away with it.

The school was okay. Lee and me were always the two that arrived late for class and because the corridors were empty, we'd nick bottles of milk and drink them quickly. We were always getting up to stuff like that. I remember one day we decided it would be fun to go for a wander around a hospital. We had a few nurses chasing us that day, despite Lee saying, "I'm looking for my mum, my mum works here." They didn't believe him.

Tracy: When we were at primary school Lee had to look after me, which gave him the hump. But he was my older brother, so that's what he was meant to do. When we were a bit older, he'd take me with him to places and we'd get up to mischief. Jumping freight trains was a favourite of ours. There was a railway line just along from where we lived in Denyer House. The trains used to slow down on that stretch, so that's where we'd jump on them. We had no idea where the trains were going and sometimes we could jump on another one and get back home, at other times they just kept on going. There were times when we got caught and taken to police stations and our parents were told to come and collect us. I remember our dad coming to pick us up and he was not very happy.

I did get sent to Mr Lendon the headmaster's office, because I got caught taking a sixpence from someone's locker. I don't recall how I got caught because I usually got away with stuff like that. The headmaster looked like John F. Kennedy and he gave me a right ticking off. There was probably relief on both sides when I moved away to Holly Lodge and another school.

Back in those days, dozens of kids actually played out in the streets. I especially loved Denyer House because of this. Outside the flats and facing Highgate Road there was a large, grassed square area, far enough away from the main road for us to feel safe as we played bulldog. We could spend hours running around trying not only to tag someone, but to lift them off the floor for a second or two. Naturally, the less robust kids always got tagged the most but it was done in fun.

Inside the horseshoe that was Denyer House, the enclosed area would be covered with washing lines where bedsheets and clothing swayed, as tumble dryers hadn't reached our shores. The mums would remove all of this before us kids returned home from school, which meant we had an area to play cricket and football, and generally burn off some energy. Parents would sit out on their balconies or throw open their windows to keep an eye on us, which people seemed happier to do in those days in case things turned nasty. Mr Woods or Mrs Bunker would keep us in check.

Not too far away was Parliament Hill Fields, located on the southern end of Hampstead Heath. Rumour had it this was the spot where Guy Fawkes intended to watch Parliament blow up on November 5, 1605. He would have needed a long line of gunpowder! But on a clear day, one could go on a hop, skip and jump to find the best views of London and its forever changing skyline.

Next to Denyer House was an area that had been bombed in the Second World War, which the locals called Tammo Land. At one time an electrical plant had stood there, which was of enough interest to the Germans for them to bomb it. Although the Luftwaffe did eventually succeed in destroying the plant, it appears they had needed a few attempts as unexploded bombs were discovered when permission was granted to start building the Ingestre Road Estate, around 1973.*

My friends and me spent hours playing on Tammo Land. One of our favourite things was to build camps, just beside the rail track that was used solely for freight trains.

---

* I had a conversation on Robert Elms' radio show about how Tammo Land got its name. It turned out that some wealthy Dutch guy called Tammo, who by all accounts was a bit of a bohemian, approached the London County Council, requesting that the land be handed over to the local children as a play area.

Our camp would thunder and vibrate as the freighters rumbled by. We'd turn up with our next meal, which consisted of Smiths crisps, sherbet bonbons and bottles of Zing, like highwaymen with our spoils. It always felt like an achievement to build a camp, and then we'd just sit around in it, chomping on sweets.*

Mike Barson: As kids we found plenty to do in our local area. There were also plenty of characters. One was Mr Wynn, who took pleasure in chasing us away from the 'rods' [railway lines] that we liked to mess about on. We turned the areas that we lived in into our playgrounds and we'd explore them. Railways were the out-of-bounds areas that carried a sense of secrecy about them. So we were always going to investigate.

It was exciting for us. When everyone else was walking around the streets, we were exploring the other worlds we called the rods and building camps in areas that no one ever seemed to go into. But we weren't supposed to be hanging around the railways and Mr Wynn took it upon himself to see us off, which often meant climbing over walls to make our escape.

Another of my favourite pastimes was jumping over the fence and placing pennies on the track. I'd then jump back over and wait for the train to come. Once it'd passed by, I'd

---

* My nan told me you could use soot to brush your teeth. Fact. But when I brought home a bag of coal dust from the rail track, my mum screamed at me, "Get out the house with that filth!"

retrieve the penny that was now as flat as a pancake. Obviously, our parents were never told about this.

We'd also find the odd dead fox, cut off its tail and tie it to one of our bicycles. This was the mid-60s so we'd probably seen the mods with their Vespas and Lambrettas, with fox tails hanging off the back.

I can vividly remember my dad having a tough task trying to teach me how to swim. He took me over to the lido on Parliament Hill to do that.

The lido was another of my playgrounds. I was forever getting into scrapes over there. Back when I was twelve, I received a direct punch to the mouth in a row over a rubber ball, resulting in a fractured tooth.*

There was always plenty to do over Parli Hill. In between the first and third ponds there was the 'all male' pond, where people used to walk about naked. We'd go in and have a drink from the water fountain there, just to have a peek – it was very strange.

Further up was the ladies' nude pond, where we'd peer through the bushes to catch glimpses of people's naughty parts. We were the kiddie peepers. Sometimes we'd jump over the fence just to catch the attention of the parks guards and then we'd have to make a run for it with them hot on our heels. It really was nature's playground.

---

* It stayed firm for fifty years – pretty strong bones. It only started to wobble after that, so it had to go. It was my favourite tooth, I wanted to mount it and put on my window ledge but the dentist put it in the hazardous materials box and it was gone forever.

Tony Hilton: I can remember playing football with Lee at school on a pitch that was on a complete slope and totally useless. It was on the lido side of Parliament Hill. The goalmouths were mudbaths that became frozen solid in the winter when we were usually taken to play there. In the 1960s, footballs were made out of hard leather and if the ball was in the air it was like heading a meteor. So many of the kids ran away from the ball rather than receive it, which somewhat defeats the object of the game. If by any chance you did happen to head the ball, you were likely to have the laces imprinted on your forehead.

Looking back now, the grassed areas of Parliament Hill and Tammo Land were my playgrounds and I have fond memories of them. Places like those indirectly found their way into my song-writing with Madness, because that area, NW5, was of such importance to me. It was the site of my humble beginnings.

On our birthdays, Mum always tried to get Tracy and me something that was better than the rest. When I turned ten, I got the latest black leather shoes by Tuff, which had a compass imbedded in the side. I would wear them here, there and everywhere. Mum was happy, and I was thrilled, though I would outgrow them the following year. But her generosity came at a price: on a few occasions, we would have to stay silent and hide when the bloke from the Prudential called on a Friday to collect payments loaned to families.

We were always trying to make ends meet. This followed my family around throughout my formative years, even when we moved up to Holly Lodge – a very middle-class, four-storey, Tudor-style, turn-of-the-last-century block of rented council flats – the dysfunction continued.

Holly Lodge wasn't far from Denyer House, but it was what we called the posh area. At one time the properties had been owned by Lady Workers' Homes Ltd to cater for single women moving to London to work as clerks and secretaries. But over time the buildings fell into disrepair and the London Borough of Camden took over the lease.

So the Thompson family found ourselves moved into one of the properties on the estate, 18 Langbourne Mansions. Oh yes, we'd arrived! Mum was now like a Hyacinth Bucket, kitting the flat out in very 1970s furnishings (even though we were just into 1967). Dad would acquire the funds – though within six months of settling in, he'd be away again working on the rigs! So we moved from Denyer House, which was a mid-30s, four-storey council block of many Irish families and people like us, with very little money and few prospects – not that I knew or cared about this as a ten-year-old boy. Most of the flats in Denyer House were overcrowded. In our place there were seven of us all crammed in and it was only a two-bedroom flat.

We couldn't believe our luck. This was a private estate and a gated community, one of the first of its kind in London. The buildings looked spectacular. The streets were wide and there were trees lining them, and as the estate had been built on a hill there were some incredible views of the city to be had.

Not long after moving into our new posh home, I got myself a morning paper round and my route included the homes on

Holly Lodge: Langboune Mansions, Makepeace Mansions and Oakeshott Avenue. So now I had for the first time in my life my own bedroom and a job – which meant I had some money of my own. I was thinking that we'd all made it.

The only drawback was the other kids who lived on the estate. Compared to me they were a different breed, so at first we didn't really have much to do with one another besides squaring up. But in time I did make some friends and we all found our common ground. Life was certainly on the up.

Just like any area, NW5 had its unique characters. One was an elderly tramp with a white, wiry beard that everyone called Snowball. He wore a flat cap whatever the weather, made of leather and smothered in grease. Old Snowball also wore a coat all year round, made up of several other pieces of coats. There were so many layers that they made him appear huge and monstrous.

Snowball was part of the fabric of NW5 and he was accepted because he never bothered anyone. The most us kids would get out of him was a grunt and sideways glance. It was all very harmless and we didn't tease him either, because he looked quite intimidating. Every day he'd patrol his territory, which started at the top of Highgate Hill and stretched to the bottom, near to where the Forum music venue is today. And then one day he was gone.

Another tramp was a fella called Yorkie. There are some photographs that exist of him in history books about the Highgate area. Yorkie never accepted any handouts; he'd taken a position where he wasn't going to accept anything from anybody. He built himself a shelter out of a couple of benches, outside a block of flats called Haddo House, and people left him to it. Just like Snowball he contributed to the Highgate community in his own unique way. We liked him because he looked like some old sailor – I could compare him now to Uncle Albert in *Only Fools And Horses* because of his big white beard.

When I was in Madness, I'd still see him hanging about Highgate and stop to have a chat with him. He was still giving away 5p pieces to the local oiks too. In the mid-80s, the council moved in and smashed his shelter down. Yorkie was no longer part of the community.*

To me as a kid, the hub of the Highgate community was Charlie's Fish and Chip Shop. Many Friday nights started off with a trip to Charlie's and then it would be rush home, grab a chair before anyone else, unwrap the fish and chips on your lap, and sit and watch *The Avengers* or *The Prisoner*. Once your tea was shovelled in, snuggle up to Mum and continue to watch the box.

I don't remember sitting around watching the telly much with Dad – I suppose because he wasn't around that much. I do recall spending time together as a family at Christmas and Easter in Great Yarmouth. I've got loads of memories

---

* The area has become very gentrified in recent years. Another local native is Pat McCarney: *I was recently stood outside The Bull & Last with Lee, chatting, when we were asked to move to another outside area due to neighbours complaining of the noise… on a Sunday afternoon. After four or five brief chats with the barman, the assistant manager and a manager who threatened to call the police, we respectfully informed him that if we stood 18 inches away from the public house, we would be on public ground. Citizen Partricus McCarnicus told him, "Go away!" How dare they infringe our civil liberties like that? Twats!*

of trying to stay awake on Christmas Eve, just hoping to catch Father Christmas coming through the window. We didn't have a chimney stack back at Denyer House but I knew people came in through windows.

I could never quite stay awake long enough, but once my eyes were open I'd leg it downstairs to be met with pillowcases rammed full of presents. As the morning unfolded, other members of the family would appear and there was a lot of joy and excitement. As the day rolled on and more family arrived, the house would become ever more lively and smoky and boozy. It was fantastic!

Tracy: Family was important to us. At times like Christmas, when Dad was often away, Lee, me and our mum would go to Great Yarmouth. That's where a lot of Dad's family lived. We'd stay with our grandmother and all the uncles, aunties and cousins would come around and there'd be a party. My nan knew how to put a good spread on. The food would be placed on a long table and there'd be loads of presents around a huge Christmas tree. Our Christmases were really good times. We had a strong family network when we were growing up and that was fantastic.

Great Yarmouth in the summertime was a place full of energy and vibrancy and flashy lights and weird sounds. I loved it! We stayed at our nan Doris's house on 5 St Nicholas Street, which was a stone's throw from the sandy beach. I spent many hours mucking about in the sand and in the sea. And then after a day of fun, everyone would congregate at The

Red Lion, a pub which some members of my family took over many years later.*

Back home in London I was always surrounded by family members, especially on my mum's side. The Scannells lived around Caledonian Road – I got on well with my cousins Lorraine and Connie, who'd come over to Gospel Oak on the Dream Line. We were into the same music and fashion, to a point, but the best thing was they had friends that were very attractive and quite forward, which was all very different to me. I was a virgin and like a dog on heat!

NW5 kept me alive.

We were just street kids enjoying life and the freedom that kids had back then. The streets provided us with an education that the teachers at school could never achieve. On the streets we'd learn to get along with other kids, some of them older, and we had a knack of getting into mischief, which made life interesting and fun.

We could be very naughty at times. My elder cousin told me he'd noticed a house opposite where the curtains hadn't moved for a few days and no lights had been switched on. He suggested we might go and have a nose around. We climbed in through the bathroom window, probably making enough noise to wake up the entire street, and made our way into the front room. I remember flicking the lights on and off, I suppose to make sure no one was home. We were just being

---

* I went back to The Red Lion in 2007. I ambled up to the bar and ordered a drink and there was my uncle and auntie. They stood chatting away to me for several minutes but had no idea who I was. Once I reminded them, they were delighted – "Ooh, the Madness pop star!" – and we continued our conversation as family members.

nosey really, but then we walked into the bedroom and to our surprise found two adults, a man and his wife, lying in the bed. They were both as still as anything and had eye-pads on.

But they heard us and jumped up. We were gone, out of there as fast as we could. I think we both went back out through the bathroom window at the same time – thankfully, we were both small-framed. I was only ten years old and felt sick with nerves. We never got caught but afterwards I knew what we'd done was absolutely stupid.

Another favourite pastime was breaking into telephone boxes. We didn't actually break the mechanism but dismantled it. The new, grey-coloured systems were replacing the old, black, A-B clunking machines in time for the introduction of decimalisation, and Edward Heath was again pushing his mission for the UK to join the European Economic Community. The new mechanisms would take shillings (5p) and florins or two-shilling pieces (10p). It took some effort to prise open the bit the coins fell into but we always managed to do it. Weighed down with a pocket full of coins, it would be clothes-shopping time.

Tony Hilton: During this period, aged between eight and eleven, we used to steal pushbikes. One kid would have seen a bike somewhere, usually in a knobby road, and a small gang of kids on pushbikes would ride out to the location with one kid riding pillion. That kid would ride the stolen bike back to the dingy, dirty, dark depths of the pram-shed area situated underneath the flats.

Then the bike was dismembered by all the kids with box spanners. After a few minutes, all that was left was the bike frame – although someone would have that too, of course. These scenes were not unlike vultures around a carcass in a wildlife programme. From these misadventures, each kid acquired the skill to strip a bike down to the last wheel bearing. The pieces of stolen bike were added to our own or used to make up new bikes to sell on. In fact, I can remember that my first pair of Levi's came from the proceeds of such a sale.

Because I was playing out on the streets from an early age, getting up to no good came naturally to me and my mates. Just to the side of Denyer House was a garage with one of those old roofs made of asbestos, or something similar. You had to be careful up there; we knew we needed to step on certain areas and avoid others. If there were bolts sticking out then it was safe because there'd be a beam underneath it, so it was a strong area.

Climbing up there was always fun until one of my friends, Graeme Gannon, had an accident. He stood on one of the glass safety windows and went right through it, landing on concrete below. He was unconscious and an ambulance came and took him away, pronto. A few weeks passed until I saw him again. His injuries were intense but he was recovering well – though he was part mummified and had two enormous black eyes, looking like he'd just gone the distance with Muhammad Ali. He made a full recovery, but we didn't hang around with each other after that!

Paul Catlin: Lee would climb up anything. If he saw a tall tree or drainpipe, it was like he had to have a go. He was like a squirrel, he had no fear. I remember he got caught once trying to break into the Music Machine [in Camden Town]. The security saw him but instead of giving up and climbing down to meet them, he decided to continue to climb upwards. And he kept going up, up and up. He got so high that the security decided to just leave him to it. It would have been a long fall if he'd slipped.

After leaving Gospel Oak, I went to Brookfield's School, which was on Chester Road. I was there from 1967 to 1969. My form teacher was Miss Durham. We didn't get along too well and on one occasion she made me sit in the bin. I was always finding interesting stuff that intrigued me and one time I found a magnet. I took it to school to mess around with and placed it on the side of a reel-to-reel tape recorder. I didn't know the effect it would have: I managed to erase most of what was on the tape, leaving only crackly noises. As a result, Miss Durham made me sit in the bin in front of the class for the entire lesson. Nasty bitch.

I was never really the same after that. I did know where she lived and felt an urge to put something smelly through her letterbox, but in time I got over it. It was meant to be humiliating but it actually hurt, because as the lesson went on I slipped deeper into the bin and it rubbed against my skin. Every time I relaxed a bit I got sucked in further. I was quite sore by the end of the lesson and by the end of the day I had a load of blisters around the thigh and buttock area – fucking painful.

But of course, I didn't learn any lessons. I knew the next day would be just as interesting, with a new creative punishment heading my way.

Brookfield, like most schools, was crazy in many ways, and had even crazier kids. There were two brothers called Gary and Danny Wootton who were always getting into trouble. During one playtime, the younger brother, Dan, got into a fight and every kid in the playground circled around the two of them, chanting, "Fight, fight, fight!"

Suddenly, just as the fight was getting more vicious, the older brother leapt over the cheering bystanders like some sort of superhero and jumped on his brother's assailant. It was quite a spectacle as he started beating up the older brother of the other kid too. I have no idea who started it but it didn't matter to us. We just liked any opportunity to stand around yelling, "Fight, fight, fight!"

There was a teacher at Brookfield's called Miss Coram. She was very 1960s, completely looked the part: the glamorous, sensuous 60s type you saw in the films of the day. She had the hairstyles, the make-up and the miniskirts. She was extremely sexy. I'm sure many of the male teachers tried their luck with her.

She caught me looking through the keyhole at a girl called Julie, who was being given a dressing down. Julie Brown was the hardest tomboy in the school. If you had a run in with her then you gritted your teeth; she was a jaw-breaker. But I liked Julie because she was a bit like me – forever outside the head's office.

The headmistress came out just as Miss Coram was telling me off and started to tell me off too. Her preferred choice of punishment was to slap us kids around the back of our legs and she'd muster so much power that her slaps really did hurt. She'd always manage to hit the fleshy area behind the knee – that was a pain I have no words to describe, and she knew it. The old cow!

When I got home, I'd have to tell my mum how my day had been and I'd explain what trouble I'd been in. She'd have her say and on the few occasions when Dad was home, so would he. But as I got older, I suppose I did take on some of the responsibilities of the man of the house. To some extent I became the breadwinner. And I needed to do that by whatever means – although not anything near my dad's level.

My dad didn't want me to choose a career like his and my mum especially didn't. It was only as I got into my teens that things started to change. I can recall exactly when my dad's attitude altered, because he could see what path I was heading down and he needed to teach me a thing or two – mostly about being able to lie.

But when I was a kid my parents didn't encourage me at all. There was an occasion when they made me return to a shop where I'd stolen some sweets. They had seen me licking a lollipop and asked me where I'd got it from, as they knew I didn't have any money to buy sweets. I got a right telling off for that and was made to do the walk of shame. I really did feel shameful, it truly hit home, but it wasn't going to deter me in the future.

I don't suppose it's what people expect to hear, but I didn't grow up in a musical family. All the time that I lived with Mum and Dad and Tracy at Denyer House or Holly Lodge, we never had music playing. Lots of families had radios playing or the parents played records, but we had no radio and my parents had no records. I don't even recall the family sitting around the telly watching *Top Of The Pops*.

But as I got a bit older, my interest in music increased and I got my first stereo. I actually acquired it off the back of a lorry. Once I had my stereo I was off, there was no holding me back. I had money in my pocket because I had a paper round, so I went out buying records.

I'd sit around my bedroom singing along to them. The very first songs I learned all the words to were Clarence Carter's 'Patches' and 'In The Ghetto' by Elvis. These were closely followed by 'Lola' by The Kinks – a song I suggested Madness cover for *The Dangermen Sessions* – and Jimmy Cliff's 'Vietnam'.

With my wages I bought a little radio that I could listen to as I delivered the newspapers. From 7am Radio 1 was a godsend, with Tony Blackburn and his barking mutt, Arnold. I couldn't get Radio Caroline but Radio Luxembourg was great, as this would have the week's first chart positions (208 Hit Pick). The first song I ever heard on Luxembourg was 'Pictures Of Matchstick Men' by Status Quo. I thought the intro was amazing.

Luxembourg also played a lot of Motown and records from the great soul artists of the era. This opened up my world to music on a whole new level, and I suppose it sowed the seeds of wanting to be involved in it. In some way.

2

School Days

Imet Debbie Fordham in my first weeks at Acland Burghley. We didn't get off on the right foot though, because she pulled the tassels off my brand new loafers.

I loved those shoes and had only recently gone from having to wear soppy Wayfinders, with the compass in the sole, to find my way around! I'd bought the loafers from Brick Lane for thirty bob and had been so excited when I took them into school to show them off.

Debbie: My first memory of Lee is seeing him strolling across the playground towards me and my friend Paul Douglas. Paul noticed that Lee was carrying a shoebox and I asked what was in it. Lee held up the box. I pulled out one of the loafers by the tassels and that's when they broke off.

I hadn't intended that to happen, it was an accident, but I could see that Lee was livid with me. Paul stepped in and offered to help, which meant taking the loafer and tassel to the science room and gluing them back on. Despite Paul's efforts the loafer was never the same again, but he did try, bless him. He'd be killed serving in Afghanistan many years later.

Acland Burghley was a newly built school and in its time it was considered state of the art. By the time I started attending it had only been open for three years. As soon as you walked in there were three sets of stairs that led up into the main areas. There were six classes in every year, so that gives you some idea of how big the school was, and a structure too: upper, middle and lower. There was also a system of classes one, two and three, each with two classrooms full of pupils. The so-called brighter kids were in class one and the thicker ones were in class three. You can guess which class I was in.

> **Debbie:** I think they must have streamed the kids based on what they thought they were good at. Lee's class seemed to have the kids in it that were good at art. Along with Lee there was Tony Hilton, and the teacher's name was Miss Cooper. It wasn't just art though. Lee's class got taught Spanish and my class was taught German.

Acland Burghley had a reputation of being a bit rough. I don't know if it felt like that to everybody though. There was a real mixture of pupils too, which I wasn't used to.

> **Debbie:** Acland Burghley was one of the more multiracial schools in the area. I can actually remember the

headmaster standing up in assembly and telling everyone the school would be getting some 'boat people', and he was elated because it meant the school had another nationality to boast in its ranks. It turned out that there was a brother and sister who had come to England from some war-torn country. They were both put in my class and I felt really sorry for them. They couldn't speak any English either, so they really struggled to fit in.

Having many different kinds of people was an eye-opener for many of us, as it meant you could have friends who were Greek, or Turkish, and we all treated each other the same.

Acland Burghley did have its racial problems though. A lot of the black kids would have run-ins with other pupils. It was mainly the girls that caused the problems. Some of them kicked up a stink because they wanted their own common room. They wanted to set up an 'only blacks allowed' area. They argued that they wanted to play *their* music. Debbie was outraged by that and would go into their common room because she said she liked the music they played.

Back in those days there were tensions and pupils voiced what they were worried about. It was a time of protest too. One week it would be protesting against having to wear a school uniform, and the next week it would be protesting against not being allowed to wear one. Anything and everything was a target for protest.

Debbie: Most of the teachers were young too. I suspect many were only just into their early twenties. They would have longish hair and bells hanging around their necks. There was an occasion when my mum got called up to the school, and I recall her telling my dad when we got back home that she couldn't tell who were the pupils and who were the teachers.

Paul Catlin: As Lee and I got older, I ended up going to a different school. He went to Haverstock but that didn't work out. I don't think he liked it there, so I told him to come to my school instead. The next day he showed up at Acland Burghley, strolled into a class and a teacher looked up and asked who he was. "Thompson, Miss," he replied. She told him that his name was now in the register and from that day on he attended Acland Burghley. It was a fantastic school, modern too, so there were nice science, literature and art wings.

Tony Hilton: In 1969, I started secondary school at Acland Burghley Comprehensive and I had no idea that on my first day in class I would be placed next to none other than Lee Thompson himself. Pupils at Acland were streamed according to their perceived ability or intellect and were divided into blatantly obvious upper, middle and lower groups. Typically, Lee and me found ourselves in the lower stream, which basically meant we were seen as a pair of fucking dunces.

At the time, we were both very much into the skinhead thing and were clad in Levi Sta-Prest, Ben Sherman's, Crombie overcoats, DMs and loafers, etc. Another thing we had in common was drawing. Our exercise books were decorated with artwork rather than the schoolwork they were meant for. I once noticed Lee had written the words of the two Kinks song 'Lola' and 'Apeman' in his exercise book, much to my disgust as I was still into my Trojan reggae stuff. To be honest, I thought he had gone all hippy on me.

However, we remained good friends until Lee was whisked off to do a stretch in approved school and we lost contact for a short while until about 1973/4, when we were both going to the infamous Aldenham Youth Club in Kentish Town. Things had changed a bit by then – the whole skinhead/suedehead movement had disappeared. Some kids were getting into glam rock, which made me sick, and Lee was hanging around more with people like Chris Foreman and Mike Barson, while I hung out with the Kiln Place gang. Despite this difference in our social and peer-group preferences, friendship and respect remained between us and is still the case today.

Despite Acland Burghley being purpose-built with all the mod cons, there hadn't been any room for a playing field. This meant that we'd get put on coaches every Friday and driven to an area called Canons Park which was a few miles away, near Stanmore. That's where we'd go to play sports, the boys football and cricket and the girls hockey.

It was on one of the games days that I realised my days at Acland were numbered. I bunked off and this started to become the norm. I left school and made my way up through Highgate Cemetery and Waterlow Park, ending up in some cabins at a hospital. While I was there, a woman walked in and asked me what I was doing. I told her I was waiting for my mum, who I said worked there. Of course, it was all shit.

She accepted my story though, taking off her coat and putting it on a table along with her bag, then walking out of the cabin. Once I was sure she'd gone, I opened her bag and pulled out her purse. I quickly opened it and my eyes lit up as I saw the wad of cash. It must have been her savings or something because there was over a hundred quid. Bingo!

Stuffing the cash into my pocket, I legged it out of the cabin and headed back home. I didn't spend all the money on myself though. I bought things for some of my friends, like brogues and dogtooth trousers, and I bought a girl that I knew, Karen Ellis, a smock dress – I suppose I must have fancied her.

The next thing I know, I'm being escorted down to Holmes Road police station in Kentish Town by my dad and I'm placed in an identity parade.

When the woman whose purse I'd stolen walked into the room, she immediately pointed her finger at me and said, "Yep, that's the one." It wasn't hard for her to point me out because I was the only person in the line-up. It was bang-to-rights on that occasion.

I dealt with that experience okay because it wasn't the first time I'd been nicked and taken down the police station. I must have had at least a dozen court appearances by that point – for most of which I'd stood alongside my mate Bob Townshend. I was always getting into trouble between summer 1969 and autumn 1971.

I don't remember what I did that resulted in my first trip to the police station, but I do recall feeling numb and horrified. I'd been caught and that's what shook me up. I also had my mum and dad to deal with too. I was gutted that I'd let them down but I wasn't shitting myself. After all, it wasn't like my family hadn't had dealings with the police.

There were times when the police came around home, looking for me. I can see my dad now, having serious-sounding conversations with the police officer, giving me some dirty looks. He'd then call me out and I'd have to go and take what was coming, which often meant a right clump around the head. But as soon as the copper had gone, my dad would lean into me and whisper, "Nice one, son, but don't get caught." Confusing? It was.

Tony Hilton: We were never caught stealing bikes by the police around this time but, ironically, one Saturday morning we'd been playing around the flats and not behaving in a mischievous way at all. We were approached by two coppers who asked us what we'd been up to and where we'd been; we told them we'd been playing in the flats and they told us to get in the back of the meat wagon they'd pulled up in. They took us a mile away to Hawley Road in Camden, parading us in front of an old dear and asking if we were the kids that robbed her house. Thankfully, she said it wasn't us and so the coppers dumped us in Camden, about a mile from where we lived. No doubt they were pissed off because they couldn't nick us.

Paul Catlin: Lee didn't mind a bit of petty crime. If he saw an open window, he had to climb through it and see if there was anything worth having. He'd be in and out really fast. He was very skilled at that sort of thing. There were plenty of times when Lee, Mike Barson, a mate of ours called Johnny Jones and me would plan and plot things, like getting into a building or onto a passing freight train. It was like we had our own think-tank and we were all game for it.

There was a railway line near to where we all hung out. Freight trains passed through on a regular basis and we were always jumping on them. We had no idea where those trains were heading, and there were times when we ended up in places like Nuneaton and Coventry. Lee's sister Tracy and another girl, who was only about eight at the time, came along with us. Some of us got caught and were taken to a police station; the parents were contacted and told to come and collect their child.

We loved jumping on those freight trains and back in school, during metalwork class, Lee, Mike and me would make tools that we hoped would help us break into the containers that were being transported. We were always curious to know what was inside them.

Mike Barson: We were always finding new ways to keep away the boredom. Jumping on freight trains and taking trips in them was always fun. One time, me, Lee and Si Birdsall jumped on a train and went to France. The idea of going to Europe the proper way – going through the booking process and actually paying for a ticket – was never us, but jumping on a freight train to go somewhere made sense.

Whatever we did, it always involved trying to save some money. It didn't always work out though, as we kept getting caught and fined. I even worked out that if we'd paid for tickets, we'd actually have saved money.

There was one train we jumped on where, each time it passed through a little French village, a couple of the carriages would get removed. So we were on a train that was getting shorter and shorter and we had to keep moving up, hoping not to get caught. We eventually got off at Cognac, where we saw people making the wine by stamping on the grapes. We thought it was quite educational: we went to places like Paris and Dijon, and it was always an exciting adventure. We tried to reach Spain, too, but never got there.

Chris Foreman: Thommo was a right tealeaf.* He was always breaking into things and stealing stuff. He was the one that our parents didn't want us hanging around with. I remember we went into Woolworths and they sold lots of patches that we'd sew onto our jean jackets. There was a peace sign against an American flag which we stole. There was also an art shop that Paul Catlin and I went into. They sold rotring pens. I was wearing a parka and reached up, took one of those pens and slid it into my sleeve. The thrill was almost sexual. But

* Rhyming slang: tealeaf = thief.

I thought the people in the shop were really nice and I shouldn't steal from them. I felt bad about it.

It wasn't like stealing from Woolworths who we thought had loads of money. Thommo and me went into Woolworths and nicked some trainers – they weren't even any good, they were just crappy Woolworths trainers. We then went and played football on a patch of grass near some flats, until we heard the police sirens. Two or three police cars showed up and made everyone stand in a line. They had someone from Woolworths with them and they pointed us out as the ones who had stolen the trainers. Thommo and me got marched off to the police station.

There were also times when I got into trouble with the police but didn't end up in court. If the crime wasn't too serious the police just handed me cautions. I got plenty of those for silly things like smashing windows.

There were more serious incidents though, one of which did get me into some serious bother. A couple of mates and myself broke into an old lock-up in Kentish Town. Once inside, we found a racing car. We also found some greased oil guns and, for some reason, decided it would be fun to use the guns to make patterns on the car's doors, bonnet and windows. That was fun, but rubbing the oil in was even more so, and so we made a right mess.

We lost our smiles, however, when the lock-up doors opened and this huge fella stood barring our way out. He had a frightening voice too, as he shouted at us all to go and stand in a corner. We didn't need telling twice and all huddled together, cowering. He was very authoritative, which made perfect sense once we found out he was a local copper.

I didn't consider the sort of stuff I was getting up to as being wrong. I was just having fun. I think I got bored easily when I was young and it was the boredom that got me into situations. The thing was that neither getting caught, nor going to the police station or court, nor having the police come knocking on the door ever deterred me from further 'offending'.

Tony Hilton: I continued my friendship with Lee at school over the next few years, until 1970 when I was expelled for stealing from the Natural History Museum while on a school trip. After that I would only see Lee when he would turn up to my flats in Kiln Place to play. It was around this time that my mum had seen me hanging around with him and told me, "Don't bring that Lee Thompson in this house – he will have the fucking wallpaper off the walls!" She later changed this view, when Lee became famous in Madness, to: "When are you going to invite that Lee around for a cup of tea?" My mum's hypocrisy was second to none.

I had to leave Acland Burghley eventually but, during the time that I was there, I did make some friends. I had very little to do with Debbie though. She wasn't in my crowd and I wasn't in hers.

Debbie: I used to see Lee walking around the school. He'd be wearing a sheepskin and the pockets would be bulging with coins. I just used to think, 'You flash little bastard.'

Around early 1971, sheepskins were on their way out. I knew Mum's was a perfect fit for me, it didn't bother me that it was petrol blue and the thatched buttons were on the opposite side. It was warm and well fitting.

It was around that time that I became very aware of fashion and wanted to have a certain appearance. The skinhead look morphed into the suedehead/boot-boy/ smoothie style. It seemed to come and go in the blink of an eye. The authorities were to whisk me away before the end of the year, which meant the clothes you had were replaced with standard approved-school tat. But until then, lads wore dogtooth or Prince of Wales-check trousers or Levi Sta-Prest.

Footwear had to be either loafers or brogues, and of course army boots were popular too as they were staples for running in (they had rubber, not leather soles). I've always loved loafers and brogues ever since that period and Dr Martens would always find their way back onto me. Ben Sherman and Fred Perry shirts were all the rage as well. Put the shirts, the trousers and shoes all together and you had a really sharp look.

Mike Barson: The fashions and styles that we grew up around were really important to us. We mostly only saw what we were surrounded by. Lee, Chris and me lived very near to one another, so we were around the same things. We hardly ever ventured into the next neighbourhood, so our choices of style and fashion were really coming from what was on our doorstep.

Paul Catlin: Lee was a pioneer. I remember when he went out and bought some dogtooth trousers. He'd wear them with a black polo-neck jumper, and a Prince of Wales-check Harrington. He looked so sharp. He was the daddy and he had money in his pocket too. Lee was always turned out well. He had a great sense of style and could pull a look off perfectly. He showed a lot of us the way when it came to style.

Pete McGee: I've known Lee since 1968. He and I lived a short distance away from each other in Highgate. In those days the area had loads of old council flats, it was pretty deprived. One of those blocks of flats at the back of my house had a big green and lots of the local kids used to gather there to play football. It was because of those kick-arounds that I got to know Lee, but at that point it was sort of on and off because I was a bit older than him.

It was the skinhead movement that got Lee and me together. At the time the look was just coming in and the mod thing was on the way out. Lee loved it immediately. He really took to the Levi's, Dr Marten boots and Sta-Prest trousers. Harrington jackets were around too and at that time you could only get them in black – by the time the skinhead fashion had ended, you could get Harringtons in all colours. We'd go to a shop in Camden's Royal College Street to buy any colour – every colour of the rainbow. I remember that I had a pair of Dr Martens that caught Lee's eye – I paid 84 and sixpence for them, which works out at about £4 in today's money.

We had the clothes but what went along with it was the music – ska and reggae. We'd go out and buy records and exchange them amongst our group. We were lucky because there was a West Indian record shop in Finsbury Park, not too far from where we lived. They imported loads of records from Jamaica. We'd go down there on Saturdays and flick through the boxes, there was a lot that we'd never heard before.

Our parents had nothing so we went out and got paper rounds and milk rounds, and used our own money to buy the records and clothes that we wanted. We liked brogues so we would make our way over to a shop in Brick Lane to buy them. That particular shop also sold the Ben Sherman's and braces that we liked.

In 1970/71 it was very much a skinhead look. London had a lot of skinheads. It was also the time when the Richard Allen books came out. Allen, whose real name was James Moffat, wrote a series of pulp novels that became cult classics. The first was *Skinhead*, which was published in 1970. The story of Joe Hawkins sucked young kids like myself in. Moffat was a middle-aged hack who exploited youth culture and didn't spare the race hate (which chimed with his own views). Everyone seemed to have a copy of the book. Allen then followed up *Skinhead* with *Suedehead, Demo, Boot Boys, Skinhead Girls, Sorts, Smoothies...*

The book covers were really good, with images of people who looked just like us. *Skinhead* had a teenage boy propped up on a wastepipe against a brick wall, his hands behind his head, wearing braces and boots. *Suedehead* showed a lad wearing a Crombie and sharply creased trousers, with red socks tucked into his Royals (brogues). *Boot Boys* showed lads with longer hair: one wore a purple penny-collar shirt and a striped jumper (but not like my own striped tank top!). All of the covers showed the kids looking mean and menacing.

> **Debbie:** Kids could look mean. I used to go to watch Arsenal a lot and I remember the boot-boy lads there used to wear white butcher's coats, which some would paint on the back of.

I don't recall the first time I ever saw another boy dressed like a skinhead, or thought to myself that I wanted to look like that. But there were twins that lived in my area, Paul and Steve Anan, who were always turned out well in Crombies, Sta-Prest and Dr Martens. They looked the biz. There were other lads too; Micky Hearn and Pete McGee had that skinhead look down to a 'T'. When everyone seemed to be dressed in blue and grey, those lads wore colour and stood out.

It was because of older boy like them that I got attracted to the skinhead style. It wasn't long before I'd discarded my bomber jacket, denims from Woolworths and horseshoe-heeled, hobnail boots from Holts in Camden. (As my paper-round days were now coming to an end, much to the relief of the residents on the estate!) Instead, I got myself a Harrington jacket, dogtooth trousers and American patterned brogues from Chapel Market in Islington – legitimately this time. *Wallop!*

I remember seeing a poster for a film called *Bronco Bullfrog*. It showed the bottom half of some lad who wears jeans with a one-inch turn-up and eight-holed, yellow-trimmed DMs. I got to see the film too and liked the story of Del Walker and his mates, as they went on various adventures around the East End of London. Just like the kids on the covers of Richard Allen's books, *Bronco Bullfrog* had kids that looked and talked just like us and got up to the same sort of mischief. I was able to relate to it.

A Clockwork Orange was a really influential film, too, that drew on some of the skinhead style – like the Dr Marten boots and white, butcher-style boiler suits. It came out in 1972 and was directed by Stanley Kubrick. That film had a huge impact on the youth of the day. A lot of people couldn't stomach the story of Alex, his 'droogs' and the ultra-violence they got up to. Kubrick actually pulled the film after its response from the media and its impact on some people.

I did get to see it before it got withdrawn, with a few mates at the Leicester Square Odeon. We didn't pay but managed to break in through a door that led into the cinema. Once inside, we hid in the dark; then, when we got near the big curtain, we were like rats scuttling across the floor to reach some empty seats. We crouched down, then slowly eased up into the chair and sat back to watch the film.

Chalky (Madness roadie): I can picture Lee wearing these Clockwork Orangey boots that would always have different colour laces in them. He was always doing things that were different and made him stand out as an individual.

A Clockwork Orange was a game changer. It was shocking. There had been no film like it and didn't we just know it? After watching it, we walked out and made our way back to our homes feeling like we were indestructible. We felt like we had arrived. It was our time now.

I think a lot of kids my age experienced the same sort of thing. The fact that we'd even been able to see it was a huge achievement, because it was an adults-only film and we were still only about fourteen years old. We didn't become droogs and go out seeking 'the old ultra-violence' though. In truth we just carried on as usual, breaking into telephone boxes and the gas meters of the soon-to-be-demolished council blocks around Archway, London N19 and N6.

Violence was never really my thing. I could never subscribe to the 'Paki-bashing' and bullying fad that some engaged with. There were skinheads who did go through that phase, who you'd hear about through the local media, but it could be anyone. I read about a relative in a gang of 'hairies' (basically unshaven greasers without motorbikes), who made the local rag for 'gay-bashing' – a rampant event over at Hampstead Heath on summer evenings, in an area behind the Jack Straw's Castle pub. (And this was the 'Summer of Love', soon after the decriminalisation of gay practices, on black humourist/playwright Joe Orton's old mincing ground.*)

'Paki-bashing' wasn't something that all skinheads did either, though it was never a jolly experience when we had the racists turning up at Madness gigs. Maybe we'll come to that later...

The skinhead look came out of the mod look – there were a lot of similarities in items like Levi's, loafers and Ben Sherman's. And then, after the skinheads, there were the suedeheads and then the boot boys – I liked their look too, but from a distance. The penny-collar shirts were suspect: I bought a red one by Brutus along with near-see-through flares; binned them before the first wash.

Topper's were a must-have shoe. Stephen Topper had been very successful since the mid-60s and his shoes were often worn by members of groups like the Small Faces or the Rolling Stones. There were a few Topper's shoe-shops plotted around London and that included one in Carnaby Street. The shoes I liked had crepe-like soles and a patchwork pattern. They were really shiny too, so people noticed them. This was just before the glam-rock period and 'Ride A White Swan'.

Debbie: Because we didn't have much money we could only wear cheaper versions of the originals. So we'd have a two-tone skirt but it wasn't the best material and

---

* I became a big fan of Orton's after seeing the films *Entertaining Mr Sloane* and *Loot*, which would later inspire me with visual ideas for Madness videos.

it wasn't made brilliantly. You'd get a Prince of Wales-check skirt but the pattern wouldn't line up in all areas. We didn't care because that's all that we could afford.

Levi jeans and Sta-Prest were expensive. Not many of my friends wore Levi's because they were well out of our financial reach. However, there were occasions when I just went to the local telephone box to 'adjust it' and then went and bought something original.

> **Debbie:** Not having the money to buy things, I stopped wearing what the skinhead girls wore and went straight to being more of a hippy. This meant I could go to jumble sales and buy cheap clothes that I would then customise.

There was a shop on Hampstead Road called Laurence Corner. We'd go there to buy clothes sometimes. It sold army and navy surplus clothing and had been frequented by the likes of The Beatles, when they were looking for inspiration for their *Sgt Pepper's Lonely Hearts Club Band* cover.*

Chris Foreman and me brought navy/brilliant white sailor's trousers from Laurence Corner. Stiff Records later hired their military wear for Madness videos, i.e. 'Night Boat', 'Uncle Sam' and 'The Sun And The Rain'. I got a

---

* The Laurence Corner shop shut down in 2007 after the owner, Victor Jamilly, died, but they are now selling clothes again from premises in Camden Market. I drove pass the shop at the time of its closing and there was a tiny old guy sitting outside, all dressed up in old army clothes. He looked royally (and loyally) sad.

leather ammunition belt that held bits and bobs like mini-superballs, plastic noses, tin bird whistles. I'd make Scooby-Doo strings to attach to the belt, whilst hanging around on tour.*

The fashions seemed to move very quickly back then. The mod thing or skinhead thing, the suedeheads or boot boys, didn't hang around for too long. New styles were always coming and going. One minute a shop window would be full of Ben Sherman's and Fred Perry's, the next minute there would be something entirely different there, like a selection of kipper ties and flares with a buckle on the rear, or poncey patent leather winklepickers.

The thing with fashion is that the styles always come back around after a decade or so. Something like Fred Perry's or Levi's jeans never seems to go away. Teenagers from every generation are governed by how much money they have available to them. A lot of the mods in the 1960s wanted to get decent jobs that paid well because they wanted to buy nice tailor-made suits. A shirt like a Sherman was quite expensive, which is why a lot of kids wore Brutus shirts instead. Some people called the Brutus shirt the 'poor man's Ben Sherman', which it was for many of us.

But there was another shirt-maker that was even more expensive that Sherman and that was Arnold Palmer. I never

* For my first two appearances on *Top Of The Pops* for 'The Prince', I wore a suit from a charity shop, as well as for the 'One Step Beyond...' video at the Hope & Anchor. I absolutely loved the cut of it, as well as an identical one in grey-green. Sadly, they would get nicked from the 2Tone bus in Cardiff. Karma in Cardiff...

owned an Arnold Palmer shirt but they were popular with the skinheads, many with tartan designs.

Fred Perry polo shirts have always been a favourite of mine. I had a black one with yellow piping around the collar that I really liked, but in the early 70s there were only a few colours available: white with blue piping; West Ham colours were commonly worn and preferred by a lot of my mates, the claret and powder blue. Nowadays, of course, Fred Perry makes a load of different-coloured polo shirts, but it's always a Ben Sherman shirt for me.

There have been periods where I haven't wanted to follow the current trends. What I would do was make my own fashions. Tank tops were around in cotton form, in a vest shape that Mike Barson never seemed to be out of, or the long-sleeved, cotton 'scoop neck', low and wide around the neck area. I tended to feel a little naked in this but persevered, bogging out the odd mincer over the park.

But I had a special tank top: it was woollen but not itchy, so I could wear it with nothing on underneath, thereby accentuating my now blossoming physique. I wish I had a photo of it. I had ironed on a rainbow patch, which even had the pot of gold at one end. It had stripes too that ran black, red, green, yellow and then an unexpected pink stripe too. No one had a tank top like mine.

Looking back, I can see why. But at the time I thought it looked brilliant, especially when I'd wear it with my snow white Levi's – cut an inch above the top of my steel-toecapped Dr Marten boots from Blackmans on Brick Lane. I loved those boots. I'd scalpel out a sixpence-sized piece of the leather toecap and wire-brushed the steel to really bring out the shine. I think I varnished them too. They could blind you.

Debbie: I think the 1970s was a good time for creative and arty-type people. People could experiment. The first time I met Mike Barson he was wearing footwear that he'd designed himself. He'd basically stuck together four pairs of different coloured flip-flops. It really impressed me though.

Paul Catlin: Lee and me were at Acland Burghley when Bowie and Bolan were popular. It was a very exciting time for fashion and music, and everything was wide open to be explored. Lee was well liked. He was fun to be around and good looking too, fit as a butcher's dog, so the girls liked him. I think he tried to model himself on Andy Mackay of Roxy Music – he was a big Roxy fan at the time. He even had his hairstyles the same as Roxy members.

New York Dolls, Mott, Roxy Music, Bowie and the 'Glittered One' were inspirations to me. I actually took the time and the trouble to embroider some of their names in red cotton letters on my jacket. Customising my own clothes was fun to do and in the mid-70s I started messing around with my Dr Marten boots too, painting them various colours.

I met Gary Glitter at Capital Radio briefly once. I stood in a hallway in my Dr Spock loons and blue DMs and he ran toward me with open arms. I found myself doing the same in awe. He ran straight past me and into the arms of the late, great radio DJ Alan Freeman, aka 'Fluff'. I immediately wished for the ground to swallow me up. The Bacofoiled bastard! He let us all down.

I feel now that glam fashions lost it on a bend, red-lining for a head-on crash at the crossroads. The now-established mullet forced itself upon us care of Chicory Tip on *Top Of The Pops* with 'Son Of My Father'. At least Rod the Mod put a bit more style (and a few highlights) into it – button-waisted Oxford bags, at floor level so that you couldn't see the footwear. Platform shoes maybe?

Ouch! I'll confess that Chris and me did indulge for a short period, along with hair colour, but these were fashion abortions...

Tracy: Lee was really into Roxy Music and David Bowie – I think Gilbert O'Sullivan and Alice Cooper too. He'd try to dress like them and even put some make-up on. I recall him wearing eyeliner and, one time, he went on stage with some of my expensive red lipstick on. I went absolutely mental at him because that lipstick cost me about ten quid, which was a lot back in those days.

Hold up! Fortunately I'm overseeing this book – so I'll admit to eyeliner, but the lipstick? Dream on. (I might have dabbled in private, Tracy!)

Elaborate embroidery or patches were also very popular during the 70s. You could buy patches anywhere and they were really cheap. There was a shop on Oxford Street where I would go to and sift through boxes of them. Patches were also useful to literally patch up holes. There was an element of 'How long can I make these Levi's last?' Holes often appeared on the knee area and up the butt, so I'd stick patches onto those parts. I've got a photograph somewhere of me in a pair of jeans that have a leopard-skin patch sewn onto the arse.

Now you can go into a shop that sells jeans with holes all over them and charges a mint, or buy a jacket with patches already stitched on it. It's already done for you. We were happy to do it for ourselves, we had to be creative. It was a form of job satisfaction, therapeutically satisfying.

Another really important band for me was the New York Dolls. Their debut album, simply called *New York Dolls*, pictured Johnny Thunders and Sylvain Sylvain and the rest of the band huddled together on a sofa, looking very rock'n'roll, and very camp. They all had big hair and wore big 1970s shoes. The band's logo was written in a flowing style as if with red lipstick. I recreated that and embroidered it onto my jeans.

The style of Roxy Music also influenced the way I started to dress and wear my hair. For a while I even used eyeliner – this was just before I started going out with Debbie, I don't think she would have put up with it. (She probably wouldn't have loaned me her make-up anyway.)

I recall putting food colouring in my hair; Mike Barson did it too. On one occasion he put yellow in and dived into a swimming pool. You can imagine what happened.

Around the time of glam rock you could also obtain cans of silver and gold hairspray from the chemist's. You were supposed to apply it using a special head cover with holes in it. We just pierced holes in a plastic shopping bag and used that. You then pulled your hair through the holes and applied hairspray. We looked more like Rod Stewart than a member of Roxy.

Although glam rock was fashionable, we only took elements of it. We put our own spin on it. I mixed the glam look up with Dr Marten boots and jeans, then added the all-important 1950s teddy-boy hairstyle. Very Roxy, very rugged. It was flash and risky for the period; only in London could you mix the fashions and feel comfortable.

Debbie: Lee didn't just like bands because they had good songs or brilliant singers. The band's appearance and style were very important to him too. That visual part was something that Lee took to Madness. I think that showmanship was something he learned from those 1970s groups.

3

On The Beat

If Brookfield Primary was the testing ground for my truanting, it was at Acland Burghley that I really lost my taste for being at school. My first day there, I was running in the school corridor and took a full-on face slap from Miss Ward, one hard-looking lady.

Then Mr Ashby, a few months later, would kick me so fucking hard up the arse that I found it difficult to sit comfortably for the rest of our half-term holiday at Sayers Croft, near Dorking. My punishment was for dropping the school's tin milk lid. It must have been grating on him all week. I never turned my back on that swinging dick again.

Tracey Barnett: My earliest memory of Lee is from when we went on a school journey to Sayers Croft in Surrey, May 1970, where we slept in dormitories which looked like Stalags. We were treated like POWs too. I was walking to the swimming pool one day and saw Lee sitting outside the boys' Stalag, all alone with his battered little brown leather suitcase, resembling a WWII evacuee. He was on a threat to be sent home as he'd been naughty.

I went and talked to him as he looked a very sad figure, sitting there on his own. I most remember his feet – they were the smallest I'd ever seen on a boy and I felt I had to protect him. I said to him, "If anyone picks on you, just tell them I am your sister" – not that I was anyone to fear but I wanted to protect him. After that I told everyone I was his sister, and we are still great friends fifty years later.

The following summer we had a school trip to Belgium. Middle of the Road's 'Chirpy Chirpy Cheep Cheep' seemed to be constantly on the radio. One evening Lee and the boys' group made their way into the girls' room – not for any hanky-panky, just an afterhours chat. They were caught by one of the female teachers and marched back to their rooms. I later heard the sound of splashing water; as I leaned over the balcony I noticed several tops-of-heads and their cute, peeing willies.

I'd go into school in the morning, but as soon as the register had been taken, I'd be off. It was on those days that I'd usually go and meet up with Bob Townshend. He'd often be waiting for me on the island where the Archway Tavern was situated and we'd wander north/northwest within a two-mile radius. At the foot of Highgate West Hill was Ron's Café where we'd sometimes sit for hours, sipping a lukewarm stewed tea and chomping on a hot-dog roll. This was where we were allowed to count our small change and change it into £1 notes.

I knew from around this time that I was going to be academically challenged, so my chances of becoming a brain surgeon were a non-starter. Bunking off became second nature to me. I'd rather sit around in some café talking shit with Bob than being cooped up in some classroom – which I found painful, especially on hot summer days.

I'd actually started bunking off with my friend David during my last year at Brookfield Junior School; his parents ran a youth hostel association and he was a very well-spoken, curly-haired, middle-class lad. Another boy from the junior school, a very well-mannered, baby-faced, Jewish lad, was prone to dipping into his mum's purse and lifting a quid or two. But they were both nice, easy-going kids.

On those days, we'd use the money we'd pinched to go to places like Chessington Zoo and head for the ghost train, or Battersea Fun Fair (the Tunnel of Love and big dipper at age eleven? Not half!), or the British Museum. We'd travel what seemed like vast distances via Gospel Oak overground with the Red/Green Bus Rover, a daily bus pass to dreamland, two naughty kids having some unbelievable adventures.

Ah, the joys of being young, carefree and senseless! I got to see a lot of London riding a bike, hopping on a Routemaster bus or catching the Tube. It was the sense of freedom that I loved; it was just more fun than being in school. Bunking off was a means to making a difference to the day.

Bob and I would sometimes 'borrow' pushbikes and cycle around London. We'd spend the day cycling through

Regent's Park, Hyde Park or go south of the river to Battersea Park. I suppose I was having my own unofficial school trips, learning about the city that I was growing up in. I loved being just a boy in the city.

Music was also becoming increasingly important to me. It was soul that I felt attracted to, especially the music Motown was producing. The first Motown track that really grabbed my attention was 'The Tears Of A Clown' by Smokey Robinson and the Miracles. I can remember, clear as a bell, hearing that song on my paper round once school was out. At the time Tony Blackburn played a lot of soul music on his radio show. He was a much-needed champion for soul music in the late 60s and even tried his own hand at performing the songs. (He covered 'I'll Do Anything' by Doris Troy using a pseudonym, Lenny Gamble.) His singing career never really took off, but he was responsible for introducing a lot of kids to really good soul music. I came to love Motown, and it was because of him that I wanted to become a DJ myself.*

With whatever money I made from my paper round (or other means), I was determined to collect records to boost my collection, so that I'd have enough to DJ with. I loved the simplicity of reggae and Motown music. Throughout my career, whatever group I've been in, I've always had a

---

* I only met Tony Blackburn once but I must have caught him on a bad day. I bumped into him at a radio station near Leicester Square, but he was a bit moody. I asked him, "Alright Tony, all good?" but he just came back with a half-interested "Yes, all good," and carried on walking, head lowered. Debbie bumped into him recently, as he was coming out of Barnet Odeon, and found him to be very nice, even managing to get a photograph taken with him. Well jel!

Motown song or two in the set. In the early days of Madness, it was 'Shop Around' – another brilliant song from The Miracles. This was a track we learned very early on and would include as one of our closing songs, way before we'd even written self-penned tracks like 'Bed And Breakfast Man' or 'My Girl'.

Thirty years on and I'm still playing Motown tracks. At an NHS benefit gig I recently played with my son, Daley, we performed the Marvin Gaye tune 'Can I Get A Witness?' and The Supremes' 'Itching In My Heart'.

The way Motown used strings and vocals always really impressed me. There was nothing around that compared to what Motown musicians, like their house band The Funk Brothers, were creating. The Motown songwriters were special too: their stable included people like Norman Whitfield, Ashford and Simpson, Smokey Robinson and, of course, the incredible Eddie Holland–Lamont Dozier–Brian Holland.

A lot of the artists on Motown wrote for their fellow label members. It must have been a really amazing time to be in the 'Snake Pit' at Hitsville USA. What Motown achieved also inspired a lot of people to start up their own record labels. Among them would be Jerry Dammers with his 2Tone label, which also played a part in the Madness story...

The Sound of Young America was the sound of young Lee Thompson from the late 60s into the 70s. I also liked the music that other soul labels like Stax and Atlantic were putting out. Whereas Motown had the Funk Brothers, Stax had Booker T. and the M.G.'s, who played behind many of the artists that Stax and Atlantic shared at some point: like Otis Redding, Sam and Dave or Wilson Pickett. The 60s was a really creative time for those soul labels and so many of their songs got a lot of mainstream airplay here in Britain.

I also liked some of the R&B guys that had been around for a while and influenced the soul scene. I was a massive fan of Ray Charles, who'd been with Atlantic and released songs like 'What'd I Say' and 'I Got A Woman' – huge hits for him. The first song I ever wrote was based on a Ray Charles tune called 'Worried Mind'. I put my own lyrics to the song's melody while I was working on some 'oil rig' at the time. (I don't remember what I did with the piece of paper I scribbled the lyrics onto – probably threw it into the sea.)

Although I liked soul music, it wasn't something that was as popular with my friends at the time. I don't really recall my mates really being into music much at all – except Pete McGee, who introduced me to the Trojan reggae label in the late 60s. It wasn't that music engrossed me above everything else – that only happened when glam rock came along and I became friends with Chrissy Boy. This was also around the time I got interested in *Top Of The Pops*, a massively important TV programme for music-loving teenagers – and also part of Madness' history.

Alongside soul and Motown, my other musical interest was reggae and ska. Reggae was getting a fair bit of attention in the late 60s and early 70s. Tracks like 'The Israelites' by Desmond Dekker and 'Double Barrel' by Dave and Ansel Collins were hits. The song that hooked me was 'Return Of Django', recorded by The Upsetters – which was really

Lee 'Scratch' Perry. He'd had a song out previously called 'I Am The Upsetter' and had been recording loads of Jamaican artists who eventually became popular in Britain.

It was the saxophone on the song, played by Val Bennett, that I really liked. It was simple, squeaky and just right. This was years before I started to play the sax but, looking back, I suppose I did listen out for the saxophones on those reggae records. Maybe that's where the first seeds were planted.

Jimmy Cliff's music was particularly important to me. There was something about his lyrics that caught my attention, with his anti-war classic 'Vietnam', 'Many Rivers To Cross', 'Wonderful World, Beautiful People' and 'The Harder They Come' – all massively influential for kids like me.

Another stand-out group for me was Toots and the Maytals. They had broken through with songs like '54-46 (That's My Number)', 'Monkey Man' and the brilliant 'Pressure Drop'.*

---

* Toots and the Maytals came along to our House of Common concert on Clapham Common in 2016. As far as I'm concerned, Toots nicked the show that day. If there had been a roof he'd have taken it off. The crowd loved him. He was something to watch because he sang from the hip, holding his microphone really low. No one else sang the way Toots did.

I managed to spend some time with him. He could be quite difficult to understand because of his very deep Jamaican accent, but he was very nice and very humble. He was also shorter than me, and I'm only five foot and a bit, but his presence and voice made up for his stature once he got on stage.

The first time I met Toots was at our Finsbury Park comeback in '92. It was sound-check time, I looked up and noticed this black fella walking very fast towards me: "Excuse me sir, can you tell me where I can find the stage?" I was in awe but managed to introduce myself and point him in the right direction. I remember Toots was followed by a rather flustered

Reggae was very popular with the skinheads at the time. In my world it was either that or following the hippy movement. I did have some hippy friends: the Webb Family, proper bohemian eccentricity of the highest order, lived bang opposite the church on Highgate West Hill. Where you or I might take a dog for a walk, the Webbs would take their donkey and midget ponies. Barbara Webb took me under her wing, taught me my times tables and chess, and read my fortune with Tarot cards.*

But I liked the skinhead things because of the clothes they wore. And I just happened to like reggae because of the sound and feel of it.

John Hasler: Lee came up with an idea and offered us ten bob to get our hair cut like his. I agreed and we went to some place in Camden Town to get it done. I was a bit impulsive like that, plus my dad was bang onto me all the time to get my hair cut so I thought, 'This will show him.' When I went home with my number one, my old man was furious.

A lot of the reggae that came out at the time was released on Trojan Records, founded in 1968 by Lee Gopthal. The

---

young black female, one of his backing vocalists. She wasn't looking too well. I had a feeling she'd had morning sickness, or a dodgy meal. She turned out to be Toots' daughter.

* In time we drifted apart, only to find our paths cross again some thirty years later with my band Crunch! Barbara became our driver. She also fancied herself as a female Citizen Smith, a real revolutionary: "Fuck the poll tax!" "Fuck all the Tories!" Maybe she played too many chess games, but I loved her attitude. Fiery woman.

timing was perfect because this was when the skinhead movement got started in London. Trojan put out the *Tighten Up* and *Club Reggae* compilation albums, which were very popular.

It was the Trojan releases that made me want to find out more about the roots of the music, which led me to go further back into the 60s. That's when I discovered the Blue Beat label and Prince Buster. As soon as I heard Prince Buster I wanted more, seeking out and collecting his records. With songs like 'Madness', 'One Step Beyond' and 'Al Capone', you can hear how influential he was on me.

There was a shop on Upper Street in Islington, just along from the Hope & Anchor, that was full of junk. It was like an Aladdin's cave inside. In one of the corners there was a stack of records all packed inside old Schweppes boxes. The boxes were full of reggae and ska from all different record labels, but amongst them was a fair bit of Blue Beat.

There was something about that Blue Beat label, with its blue and silver design, that really grabbed me. It didn't matter who the artist was, you were pretty much guaranteed to skank to the tune. Over the coming months I purchased loads of Prince Buster records from that junk shop. Not all at one time – I had to keep returning because I only had a certain amount of money. But in the end I must have bought near-150 singles by various artists, on a variety of labels I'd never heard of before, all from that little cave.

When I started at Chafford Approved School, a lot of the other inmates there had come from London. There were quite a lot of black lads from south London – mostly from places like Brixton – who brought with them their record collections, mostly made up of Trojan. These would get played on the small mono record player in the games room. It was there that I first saw the *Tighten Up* album sleeve with a naked woman adorning the cover. It certainly drew me in. This was Volume Two in the series and the words were written across the woman's body in red lipstick, with just enough of her breast on show.

This album included 'Return Of Django', which I loved, along with tracks like 'Long Shot Kick The Bucket' by The Pioneers, a song The Specials would later cover, and 'Wreck A Buddy' by the Soul Sisters.

There were a few of those *Tighten Up*s released and Volume Six's cover showed a pretty, curvy, naked female enwrapped in a snake. The sleeve covers on all of those albums were as impressive as the songs. I've still got them at home and every track is a winner, rough and ready. There was no time for second takes or pratting around with your tuning fork. The musicians would prep in a shack and then go into the studio after doing their homework. Coxsone Dodd's studio worked to a tight schedule, while Lee Perry was a master of disregarding the odd cock-up!

I played those records until the stylus had almost melted. Oh yes, it all started in the games room at Chafford. I witnessed some very unusual dance movements.

I ended up at Chafford for stealing a purse. There were other petty crimes too, but it was getting caught for the purse that sent me to the school where they'd sort me out. I was sent at first to a remand centre called Stamford House, located in Shepherd's Bush. This was where they kept the naughty kids until they were able to send them on to permanent reform schools. They had to find one that was a suitable fit for the crime(s).

(While I was at Stamford House, Benny Hill's 'Ernie [The Fastest Milkman In The West]' was at number one. I remember learning all the lyrics.)

To my surprise, Mike Barson and Chris Foreman turned up to visit me. We chatted for what seemed only a few minutes, whereas you were given at least an hour. It was a sort of temporary escape and when they had to go, I wanted to do some kind of identity swap. (Chris was my height and frame.) I could only dream on. I'd rather not have had visitors after that – which was made easy when I was relocated, as no one wanted to travel to Ramsey in Essex!

All the kids in Stamford House were under eighteen. I was with Bob Townshend there.* It had only been a matter of time before the law of averages caught up with us and put us under supervision. After Stamford they split us up. Bob went to an approved school in Redhill, Surrey and I went to Chafford in Essex.

I was only in Stamford House for a couple of weeks. Those remand centres weren't designed to hold kids for lengthy periods. It was at the time of my fourteenth birthday, October 1971, when I started at Stamford House. I spent

---

* I met him on a few occasions in later years. The last was in a probation office in Archway. I barely recognised my mate Bobby Townshend. He died in a doss house from a burst stomach ulcer, due to a bad wrap. He had a pauper's funeral, carried in a box of timber. I sat and held hands with his brother, Andrew, to one side of me and his son on the other. And that was it. A sad end in every way.

Christmas at Chafford Approved School; it was a tough time and I found being away from home really difficult. Chafford became my new home until February 1973. It was a long fourteen months.

Chafford Approved School seemed so far away from London. Harwich, the nearest town, felt like a long way from home even though Great Yarmouth was only a hitchhike up the A12. It hadn't been so bad in Stamford House because it was in London and the rules were different. At Stamford, if you behaved you got to go home at the weekends. This meant that on Friday afternoons I could walk to the nearest Tube station and make my way back to Kentish Town. I could then spend the weekend with my family and friends, and all I had to do was make sure I returned to Stamford by 7pm on Sunday night. That was okay.

It was during my time at Stamford House that I started to peel away from Bob and spend more time hanging around with Mike Barson and Chris Foreman. Mike and Chris and I would go on to form Madness, but in the years before that we were just mates getting up to mischief. John Jones and Paul Catlin were two other mates moving in the same circles – slightly edging toward the soul-boy look, always casually smart.

Chris Foreman: Me and Mike used to have Red Bus Rover passes and used those to go and see Lee when he was sent away to the approved schools. One of those places only used to let him out at the weekends. We'd all meet up and go off thieving down the West End. At the end of it he'd have to get the train from Liverpool

Street. Lee, Mike and me would be there on a Sunday night and it would be all dark and deserted. On the platform there'd be trolleys with loads of parcels on them. They were just left there, asking for it: we used to call them the Christmas parcels, take loads of them and open them up. We'd nick all sorts of bizarre things.

Out of all of my friends, it was Mike and Chris who visited me at Stamford House. This meant a lot to me and it's something that I've never forgotten. They stopped me feeling alone at a time when I didn't really know what was going to happen next. Nothing had really prepared me for an approved school, or the reality of being separated from my family and friends. It brought a tear to my eye when they came to see me.

Mike had two older brothers. I don't recall how we met but I do remember we went to see *The Bridge On The River Kwai* on re-release, the war film with Alec Guinness and William Holden. It was through Mike's brothers that I became friends with Mike. I'm not sure why I'd have tagged along with these three kids who towered over me, but they lived near to me, just a street away off the Highgate Road. Chrissy Boy lived opposite me in an old cobblestone road that led up to the railway bridge.

Chris Foreman: There used to be these old phone boxes that you had to put coins into. You'd make the call and you had a few seconds before you had to put the coins in. What Lee would do in those few seconds is shout down the phone, "I'm down the road!" In that moment he'd be trying to tell you where he was.

Mike tells the story of how Lee used to go to his and whistle from down the road to let him know he was there. He'd be trying to avoid Mike's parents. There was a lamppost where I lived and that's where Lee would be, whistling.

Despite Mike, Chris and me living so near to one another, I hadn't really known them before. Chrissy Boy had gone to Gospel Oak Junior School, like me, but we hadn't befriended each other. I didn't know Mike because he went to Brookfield Junior School.

Even from an early age Mike was quite bohemian. There was something about him and it wasn't just his height – although this may have had something to do with it, as I've always liked tall people.

The first few times that I met Mike, I found him to be quite moody and not very talkative. I got the impression that I annoyed him really. My initial impressions of Chris were that he was a bit moody too, a very cautious boy. He kept his cards very close to his chest, so you never really knew what he was thinking or feeling.

Chris and Mike had similar traits. They were both street-wise, knowledgeable and headstrong, and this was very obvious when you spent any time with them. I was nothing like them. Where they'd hold back and survey the situation, testing the waters first, I'd just dive in. But we all got on and it was the start of a friendship that has lasted for forty years.

*   *   *

I remember arriving at Chafford Approved School and being filled with dread. I actually broke down when the realisation kicked in. As I approached the manor house it dawned on me that this was it now, I'd really gone and done it and this was a consequence of my actions. I'd fucked about too much and it had caught up with me.

When I turned up, the other kids there were expecting some kind of keen DJ. Somehow, the staff had got wind of my interest and ambition, and shared this with the other kids. Of course, they had a disappointment when I did eventually show up.

There was one teacher there that I'd get along with, who I'll call Les Dribbley. He was a nice fella – albeit a bit aberrant, I came to realise. He knew I was interested in music and we connected over this. He seemed to take a shine to me and another boy – Tim Brunning, a big, stocky-built, blond kid with a capped tooth. Thank God he got on with me, as he had a temper and would take his fist to a wall or a safety glass door – though never to a person.

There were days when Les would take us both out of Chafford and we'd explore the surrounding towns like Lowestoft or Ipswich. We'd go into record shops and musical instrument stockists, or even see a film at the cinema.

He never tried anything on, but there was one occasion when we got back about 9pm and he took us to his office. Tim and I didn't think too much about it, but while we were in there he got out a roll of Sellotape and starting binding us to our chairs. We were all having a laugh, it just seemed to be innocent fun. But I sometimes wonder what happened to Mr Dribbley.

I wrote to Chris on many occasions about the goings on at Chafford, especially in the ten-bed dormitory after the 9pm lights-out curfew. Some of the stories I heard were true and some obviously fantasised – about what crimes the inmates had done, or not done in some cases.

Chafford wasn't just for boys that had gotten into trouble. It was also a place where kids were sent to when their family couldn't parent them. Some identical twins appeared one day, due to their parents not being able to cope mentally. They were short-fused peas in a pod. The only way to tell them apart was one had a turned-up, piggy-shaped nose and the other wore NHS specs that now put me in mind of Griff Rhys Jones' ad for Holsten Pils;* he was always bruising his legs due to having no sense of direction – poor, unfortunate bastard. He had a lazy eye too, and both had hair like poodles. They left suddenly, in the dead of night.

On the tenth stroke of the local church bell, the religious sparking-up of tobacco under the covers would commence. If this was detected, the night staff would enter the dorm, military style, and order us to strip our bunks – a rare invasion of quality time. Those giggles, tears, silences, moans and groans, the smells and the odd on-demand fantasising and tugging...

Chafford Approved School was nothing like the Ray Winstone/Phil Daniels film *Scum*. There was the occasional

---

* In a doctored scene from *Some Like It Hot*, Marilyn says that she prefers men in glasses. "This could be your lucky day!" comes back Griff, ogling her down a pair of drinking glasses he's wearing as goggles.

psychopath threatening, in no uncertain terms, to "Burn this fucking hellhole down!", but there was no 'daddy' bullying his way around. There wasn't the kind of violence and abuse that is depicted in that film.

Chafford wasn't a borstal at all. The crimes that us kids had committed weren't so serious that we needed to be locked up behind bars. There were no bars on the windows at Chafford.

The school had relocated from near Brentwood in the 1930s into an old manor house called Michaelstowe Hall. It was a huge building that had once been owned by a wealthy family called the Garlands, before being sold on and eventually used as a school intended to reform naughty boys.

Their intention was sound, and at Chafford boys could learn skills like painting and decorating, bricklaying, joinery or electrics. These would take place in one of the several prefab army huts that surrounded the main house.

There were some enormous rooms inside the manor house. The attic had been converted into sleeping areas with rows upon rows of bunkbeds. The rooms below the dorms were used to teach science and technology. Then there was the social/games room, where many of the boys would gather, and a huge dining/sitting room with a TV (times: 5.30 to 8.30 sharp).

Chafford had its way of doing things. It had its rules – something which many of us hadn't much experience of, or paid much attention to. It could be quite regimented at times. We'd have to be up at 6.30 in the morning every day, though that wasn't a problem for some of us. We'd then have showers and our breakfast, before being put to work.

This was mainly cleaning. The manor house was massive so there were a lot of rooms that needed maintaining. My jobs included cleaning floors and paintwork, taking curtains down, while the wardens kept a close eye on us to make sure we were doing a thorough job. They were very good at noticing the spots that had been missed and they'd make you go back to finish the task. Schoolwork would take place at 9.30–4.30.

We had to wear a uniform of sorts. This comprised a pair of cheap jeans and a navy-blue shirt with collars and buttons that only went as low as the top of your chest, meaning you had to slip it over your head to get it on and needed a fellow inmate to drag it off. We had to supply our own shoes or black plimsolls – no fancy footwear.

During my time at Chafford, Mike and Chris became my best friends. As with Stamford House we could go home at some weekends, but this was dependent on whether you'd scored enough brownie points. If I wasn't able to go home, it felt like a lifetime of waiting. I really didn't like that feeling.

When I did get to go home, I'd see my family and spend time knocking about with Chris and Mike. There was a small gang of us. When it was time for me to return to Chafford on the Sunday evening, they often came to the train station to see me off. We'd lark about until my train pulled in. I'd then jump on at the last minute and race to get a seat by the window, so I could watch them disappearing. It was like one of those romantic scenes from an old black-and-white movie

– except Mike and Chris would be making wanker gestures at me and taking the piss.

There are a few photographs of me with Mike and Chris that were taken during those weekends. There were loads of photo booths around, especially at train stations, cheap to use at 20p a pop for four. We often squeezed into them and pulled silly faces.

It was inevitable that I'd make a friend or two at Chafford, due to the length of time I spent there. One was Martin who came from Finchley, so he lived fairly near to my manor. On one of the weekends we were allowed to go home, we decided to meet up and spend some time on familiar turf. As we were strolling around one Saturday, he suggested we go in a certain direction so I followed.

The next thing I knew, he was leaping over a fence to a building on the other side. I didn't follow him, I just waited, with no idea of what he was getting up to. When he returned he was clutching a handful of wage packets. We casually left the area to find a safe spot, where we looked inside the little brown envelopes and found £20 in each of them.

I don't know how Martin knew about that place but I suspected it was from someone he knew, or a relative even. Once he'd jumped over the fence he was in and out of that building very quickly, as if he knew what he was looking for and where he'd find it.

Once it sank in, I started to think, 'Oh fuck, what have we done?' We were on weekend leave and if we got nicked for stealing wage packets it could mean a trip to borstal. I had to learn to distance myself and avoid these situations.

Another boy I befriended in Chafford was David Bedford. He was a black fella with a comb constantly sticking out of his afro. He was bowlegged too and it looked like he walked on his heels, giving him a certain swagger and shuffle. I liked David and we got on very well. He was serious and intense when he spoke to you, but he'd got my back one time when a new arrival wanted me to be his friend – his *only* friend...

I remember David coming up and telling me I didn't need to worry about the kid any longer, as he'd been told in no uncertain terms that he'd leave Chafford a cripple if he persisted. That bullyboy kept his distance after that. I was pissed off with myself though, for resorting to pulling a knife on him – though I knew it wasn't in my nature to use it. In fact he walked towards me daring me to use it!

I missed being with my family during that Chafford period. I was surprised that I'd ended up there but I think they'd been expecting it. I remember my mum expressed to me her disappointment. I suppose my dad felt that he'd tried (up to a point) his best to keep me on the straight and narrow, but had failed. My parents thought that going to Chafford would be a lesson for me and I'd be a reformed teenager.

It kind of worked. Bob Townshend was out of the equation and I was mixing with different mates. My mum and dad also understood that if Chafford didn't work, the next stop was likely to be borstal and that would be quite a different kettle of fish from an approved school.

I didn't want borstal to take my liberty away. Looking back, I feel that being sent to Stamford House, and then Chafford, was my 'Get out of jail free card'; the timing was in my favour.

A big factor in all this was my being separated from Bob. We weren't good for each other and we were thorns in the side of the Holmes Road police, but after I'd left Chafford our friendship largely ceased. I had new friends and so did he. I did see Bob around but our friendship had been reduced to a wave from across the road. That reflected our relationship, he was going one way and I another.

I was fifteen years young when I left Chafford. It was a huge relief. I can't say I felt like that reformed character in *The Shawshank Redemption*, but it had been an experience that helped straighten me out – if only a little bit. I remember having to sit in those last meetings, to try to convince the staff I had changed. They had to feel they could let me loose into the real world. They made it very clear that they didn't want to see me again.

John Hasler: I think that approved school had a massive effect on Lee. I think he felt that he'd been stitched up and shouldn't have been sent away, I think he found it hard to trust people after that. He became quite guarded and would be cautious about who he'd let in.

Post-war, my mum stayed in the NW5 area for most of her life before having to go to Luton, Bedfordshire, and that was only because my dad had to get out of Dodge. When I was allowed to leave Chafford, I got the train home only to find that where I'd been living was no longer home.

I banged on the door but got no answer. I looked through the letterbox and saw a pile of junk mail on the floor. It dawned on me then that my family had moved but forgotten to tell me. I went to see my Uncle Jack and he told me they'd moved to Luton and gave me their new address. I was only a teenager but it was down to me to sort it.

After Chafford, I also found out that I couldn't return to my old school, where all my mates were. In fact they informed me that their policy was that once you'd left, you wouldn't be allowed to return. As a result, I ended up going to Haverstock Secondary School, which was opposite The Roundhouse in Camden.

Even though I was now going to Haverstock, I had to live with my parents in Stopsley, Luton, so I had to commute to London for my remaining fourteen months at school – God's way of telling me, "This is what you've got to look forward to!"

Getting into music; my sense of fashion; even the activities of jumping freight trains or writing graffiti on tunnels and bridges, or going to public houses – all these things would have a positive, gravitating influence on me and my mates, thankfully. But for now, although I'd turned over a new leaf, I was far from squeaky clean. The occasional clothing department or telephone box still received readjustment.

Pete McGee: Lee had a nickname for a while, we called him Tealeaf Thompson. He certainly gained a bit of a reputation for his light-fingered exploits. There were many occasions when Lee and I would go out and do little bits together. It wasn't so much about acquiring something as it was about the excitement. When Lee and me first starting going out it was the phone boxes in the area that we targeted. We worked out a way to get into the big steel box that collected the coins. We never managed to get any big money by doing this, but if we walked off with a pound-fifty we were happy.

I only ever got caught thieving with Lee once. We actually busted into someone's flat on Highgate Road. The people that lived there were Greek Cypriot and we found a load of jewellery. We took what we found but we didn't really know what it was worth. A few days later we were walking down the road wearing some of the jewellery. The Old Bill pulled over and stopped us. We got taken down the station and done for burglary.*

Mike Barson: Lee lived across the road from a launderette. There was a Mrs Curler who worked in there and we had a few run-ins with her. The launderette was one of the places we'd hang around in, because on cold nights it was warm. We'd mostly just be talking bullshit. What Mrs Curler didn't like was Lee nicking the money out of the machines. Lee was always up to no good.

It was on Saturdays when Mike, Chris and I would usually get together. We'd meet up at the launderette on Highgate Road before heading off to our intended destination of the day. We spent many a Saturday knocking about Camden Town or Kensington High Street. Our favourite pastime was

---

* We received a conditional discharge, as we were able to return all the items.

shoplifting! I'd get the blame for instigating these misadventures, but we were all to blame. I mean, you can lead a horse to water...

Sometimes we'd jump on a red bus and go somewhere, anywhere, but mostly we just bunked the Tube. It was both easy and risky, which made it fun. The London Underground network allowed us to venture anywhere; we'd find ourselves in all sorts of areas that we were unfamiliar with, which kept things interesting.

Woolworths and the Co-op were the prime targets, as they kept the vinyl in the sleeves. There's a scene in the film Madness made in 1981, *Take It Or Leave It*, where I go into a record shop called Rock On in Camden. I flick through some records and sift a batch together, then wander out only to return a little later with partner-in-crime Mike Barson.*

Mike would shield me as we'd sift a batch of merchandise under my coat, then he would do the same, leaving the shop with our coats over our shoulders in a contorted manner. It could bring unwanted attention if one of us passed wind whilst stooping down – though, thank heavens, this was rare.

But Mike and Chris were not into more serious crime, and I didn't want to be sent back to reform school. I made my last juvenile court appearance with a friend, Simon Birdsall, after a sift-up with Mike and John Jones. Mothercare, for some reason, sold Instamatic film at ridiculously high prices,

---

* Small point: this actually took place in the Co-op, Camden Town (where they also stocked Levi 501s in abundance, in sizes ranging from midgets like myself to the more lanky-legged).

so we cleared a shelf. As we waited for a bus, we saw a police car approach. Mike and JJ legged it off into a cinema; Si and myself were too slow and got caught for daylight robbery.

Simon's parents were very cool about it and we'd land up as good friends – I even became a lodger at his parents' house for a while. (I played my sax to a live crowd for the first time at Si's garden party. It was a shambles but good fun – punk was now in full swing, so we could just wing it!)

Discovering sex was another important factor on our teenage minds. There were two girls that Chris and I used to go and visit in '73, Sue and Trudy. We'd sit around, play records, drink tea and chat. Chris got off with one of the girls and I'd get off with the other. At one point we even swapped girlfriends – though it was all quite innocent fun really.

But I was starting to get an uncomfortable sensation in my scrotum. It was a swelling feeling that could really start to ache and made 'off-loading' a bit difficult. On leaving one of the girls' homes one night and strolling across Hampstead Heath, I told Chris about the feeling. I had to stop for a while because I was in agony. He listened but didn't say too much.

A few days later, as we were making our way to see the girls again, Chris asked how I'd been getting on with the aches. I told him it'd eased up. He smiled and told me he knew a remedy for it. "What's that?" I asked keenly, as it was a horrible pain to suffer. "You need to chip one out," he said. "What?!" I replied. "That's how you cure it?" "Yep, I've had to do it," he confirmed and we said no more. I soon discovered that it worked!

Later that evening, after seeing the girls, having tea, playing records and getting down to some necking, I needed to use the toilet. I had that aching pain come on again and had to try and remedy it, just like Chris had suggested. I locked the door behind me and got down to it.

Boomshakkalakka! It went everywhere, like an unmanned firehose. There was a vanity unit in the toilet with all manner of facial creams and hairbrushes stacked up. But Harry Monk* was in full swing all over the show, in uncontrollable spasms, dripping like spent candlewax.

As soon as I'd composed myself, I grabbed for the Kleenex and felt absolutely enlightened! Like a dead weight off my brain!

Amongst other interests, music was a huge factor in what glued Mike, Chrissy Boy and me together. We didn't always share a love of the same bands though. Chris was a bit of a metal/prog head and into groups like AC/DC, Hawkwind, Genesis, Alice Cooper and Led Zeppelin, which in time rubbed off on me a bit. But by 1973 it'd be the pub-rock thing that we really shared an interest in, with Dr Feelgood or, by 1975, Kilburn and the High Roads with Ian Dury. Like me, Chris was a fan of most music genres, including reggae, and we connected over that.

Mike was different again in his tastes. He was a big fan of Stevie Wonder. Traffic, Bowie, Elton John and Carole King were also important to him, what I'd call more sophisticated music. Along with reggae and Motown, it was Bowie and Roxy Music that Mike and I really connected over.

I saw a lot of groups at The Rainbow, Finsbury Park, which was easy for me to get to. The venue had been a

* Rhyming slang!

cinema back in the 1930s and 40s, but with the decline of films' popularity, groups started to play there. In the 1960s, some of the biggest acts around performed on The Rainbow's stage, including Jimi Hendrix.

During the 1970s, all the biggest groups played at The Rainbow: Bob Marley and the Wailers played there a few times; Pink Floyd and Genesis; The Who too, who honoured the venue in 'Long Live Rock'. It was there I saw Stevie Wonder; he did two nights which were attended by members of The Beatles and the Rolling Stones.

Mike Barson: We were always getting into scrapes. Our adventures often included some form of climbing up or over something. Lee and me were pretty good climbers, but Chris wasn't. Chris was always the most sensible one out of us; Lee was the wildest and I was the one in the middle. We never paid to see films at the cinema or bands in venues; we'd find ways to get in, which often meant climbing in via the roof. We went to see Stevie Wonder at The Rainbow and climbed in through a window in the roof area. We actually positioned ourselves about 100 metres above Stevie Wonder's head and watched him as he played his piano.

Chris Foreman: I remember climbing up a drainpipe onto the flat roof of The Rainbow. I looked through the window and Leo Sayer was there. He was supporting Roxy Music that night. I could see Lee and Mike below me. They were on the pavement and there was a big bouncer looking up at me and shouting, "Get down here, you little fucker!" But I was too scared to climb back down and even asked him if he could catch me.*

There was a guy Lee and me knew called Mark and we'd see him around at gigs. He could get in anywhere. I remember being at The Rainbow with him and we were at this big door which he managed to open. Once I got through it was like a maze inside. A lot those old venues, like The Rainbow or the Brixton Academy, have lots of fire escapes and I was running through them. Alex Harvey was playing that night, who I really liked. I ended up in the bar and he was in there, so and there was a quick "Alright? I really like you!"

Bowie performed at The Rainbow as Ziggy Stardust. I was a huge fan, but skint. Bowie's security was airtight that night, so I had to leave, defeated and distraught. I also caught him promoting *Aladdin Sane* at Earl's Court Olympia, with Chris. We got in the backdoor for that one thanks to a big bloke.

Seeing Bowie performing 'Starman' on *Top Of The Pops* was enlightening. I remember being blown away, not so much by the arm around Mick Ronson, but by the shy punter in the tank top behind them. That should have been me... It was a *wow!* moment. Chris used to go out with a

---

* Dream on, Chris. It was me who witnessed Leo Sayer putting his slap on – I can still see that godly being before me vividly. He had that clown kit on, with a small make-up sponge in his hand, about to buff his cheeks. Period!

girl from Seven Sisters and I'd often tag along – we'd play a lot of Bowie round her house, particularly *Hunky Dory*. 'Kooks' made me smile with every turn.

I visited a record shop on Junction Road, Archway, and asked if they had any copies of Bowie's latest album – *The Rise And Fall Of Ziggy Stardust And The Spiders From Mars*. The salesman looked at me and pointed to an area of the shop where the racks were filled with *Ziggy Stardust*. The artwork looked really impressive, so it was time to sample the content. I went home and played it over and over again. From that moment on I was a total Bowie fan, hook, line and sinker.

Chris Foreman: We were all into music. I've always been very eclectic and into all sorts. There was a lot of music in the 1970s and I think we grew up in the best era. We had Motown, reggae and glam rock. There was some incredible stuff coming out, and a good mix of genres. I remember Lee and me would go and steal records just because we liked the look of the cover.

There was a band called Split Enz who wore make-up and looked really mad. There was Bowie too. Lee and me bunked into Earl's Court on May 12, 1973 to see him. We were outside trying to work out how we were going to get in. We saw some geezer, really big and strong, and he pulled a door open. We all piled in, but then we had to get to the area where the bands played.

I remember we saw Lee's cousin Lorraine there and said, "Where's your make-up?" Thommo and me had put all this make-up on which made us look like proper

Bowie fans. We waited for the big cheer and then ran through.

This was towards the end of the Ziggy Stardust period. It was brilliant, but I remember thinking the sound wasn't very good and you couldn't hear Bowie's guitar.*

* Madness supported Bowie on September 9, 1983 at Anaheim Football Stadium, California. I'm rarely starstruck but I was when I actually got to meet him. I was in a hire car with Debbie, Suggs and his wife Anne, and we'd got lost trying to find our way into the stadium. There was a bit of a panic on because we were already running late. When we finally found where we needed to be, we all jumped out and rushed around trying to find a drink. I felt the need to calm down, so I went back outside to get some air and have a cheeky cigarette.

As I did, a couple of limousines pulled up in front of me. I watched as a small fella got out of the car dressed in a green jumpsuit, with a full head of peroxide-blond hair. He approached me with his Brixton bowl and enquired, "Excuse me, do you know where I might be able to find the Madness band?" I was dumbstruck, which is not me normally. It all seemed to be in *sloo-oo-ow motion*, not real time. I quickly pulled myself together and had a brief conversation about how the tour was going, finding him to be very humble. He then wandered off to say hello to the rest of the band.

Madness went on first. We opened with 'Madness' and closed with 'One Step Beyond…'. The other support act was The Go-Go's, an all-female band that included Belinda Carlisle, from California. I believe we walked onto the stage and announced we were playing the gig in 'order of the pineapple'. There seemed to be pineapples in abundance in all the support bands' dressing rooms at Anaheim, so we decided to take them to the stage – as if to offer them up to our gods as a sort of gift, like the Balinese do with small pots of incense, flowers and fruit.

The gig went really well and the audience were fantastic. It was certainly the biggest that Madness had played by that point. While we were in America, we also supported REM and The Police. I didn't get to see The Police and I only briefly met drummer Stewart Copeland. It was a bit of a backstage rush at the time, so I never met Sting.

I know Suggs did though. He once leapt unsteadily onto the stage in Henley while Sting was performing, to express to the audience how much he loved him! The security had to escort Suggs off, getting him more publicity than the gig itself. Classic – mission accomplished.

Another group I really liked was Mott The Hoople. I'd been a massive fan since I'd heard their debut single, 'Rock And Roll Queen', and Chris introduced me to their early albums. Mott was a lads' band, I see them as being punk before punk. I wish I'd seen them live but I never managed to.*

Chrissy Boy, Mike, Si and I tried but we didn't manage to get inside The Rainbow. All we could do was listen to them from afar. On that particular night we got caught and marched out before we managed to merge with the paying crowd. The group were promoting their 1973 album *Mott* at the time – which had 'All The Way From Memphis', with Roxy Music's Mr Andy Mackay guesting.

'All The Young Dudes' was the song that really turned me onto the band. Bowie wrote that song and produced it too – at a time when everyone loved him. It was just in the nick of time for Mott, because the group was on the verge of being dropped by Island Records and splitting up. But it was a massive hit and their first release on CBS. (Before Bowie came along, the group already had several albums out on Island – Guy Stevens produced them, many years before he did The Clash's *London Calling*.)

Debbie: Lee never paid to get into venues. He'd always try to bunk in. Lee had a certain route that he used to get into The Rainbow. It involved climbing in

---

* Well, only in later years, with friend Si Birdsall at Mott's Hammersmith Odeon reunion gig. We got thrown out of the venue's hospitality room, for serving ourselves as the bar staff had gone AWOL. That's hospitality millennium style.

through the roof area that was directly above where the groups played.

The problem with going through the roof at The Rainbow was that once you were above the group you couldn't actually see them, all you could see were the punters below. It was absolutely filthy up there when I was treading the beams with Mike, Si and Chris. But we liked the buzz of trying to sneak in rather than having to pay, plus tickets were expensive back then – all of two quid.

The route from the roof down into the auditorium meant navigating our way through a load of restricted areas. All the time we had to be quiet and keep our eyes peeled. By the time we merged with the crowd we'd be covered in dirt and grime. We must have looked like extras from *Oliver Twist*.

I got to see many top bands at The Rainbow. However, for me, the more intimate the experience the better. I'm not a festival lover – unless I'm performing there!* One of my inspirations, Alex Harvey, played the Reading Festival in '74. I was invited along by all the boys, but I was waiting for him to play London in a 300-capacity.

*　　*　　*

I maintained a firm friendship with Mike, Chrissy, Paul Catlin and JJ. We also had a new meeting place at the Aldenham Boys Club on the Highgate Road, a youth club where kids within a two-mile radius would congregate and talk over a

---

* I've been thrown out of three festivals in recent years over some pointless kerfuffle – just too much battening down, red tape, etc.

variety of topics – like 'that boy' or 'this girl', fashion, music, bands, sex and the main bone of contention, football.

Race was never an issue, which felt comfortable among the company I mingled with. If race did rear its ugly head, Black 'Dolly' Dolphis, Eddie Joseph or Pat McCarney would nip it in the bud. It made for an 'all together now' atmosphere.

I would have found the Aldenham a trifle intimidating just turning up on my own, without a recommendation from a regular. So I'd slick back my hair and stay with my uncle at weekends and head back to Luton on a Monday after school. A torturous, door-to-door, two-hour journey – though I'd eventually spend more time in London.

When my uncle Jack Scannell split up from his wife, he moved in with his dad; when my grandad passed, Denyer House was handed down to him. I decided to go back down to London and move in with Uncle Jack. It made sense as I went to school nearby and had another year to do.

Between leaving Chafford in February 1973, starting Haverstock School in Chalk Farm and leaving Haverstock at Easter '74, I stayed most of the time with my uncle. In time I'd squat in several places in the Camden area, which was never a problem back in mid-70s London.

The Aldenham opened on Monday to Friday evenings. The streets in the area were emptied of teenagers then, including locals like me, Pete McGee, Tony Hilton, Chris, Mike and Deb.

Pete McGee: That was a great place for youngsters. We had two snooker tables, a live music room, a jukebox, an area to play football and pinball machines. It was a charity-funded place and it was in there that we started meeting people who were from slightly further afield, like the top end of Kentish Town, Somers Town, Kiln Place and Queens Crescent. A lot of us became friends and we still are today.

It wasn't even that there was that much to do there, but it was our little club and when you're that age, you can just idle the time away chatting bollocks, blowing bubblegum and taking the piss out of each other over a lemonade.

There was a rooftop five-a-side football area, enclosed in a big metal grill fence to keep the footy fanatics in – fanatics like Mick Mahoney, who'd lovingly have taken a bullet for Millwall or his beloved Glasgow Rangers. Beneath the pitch was a sports hall. This catered for a range of activities like netball and basketball, rounders, badminton, tag relay or gymnastics. It was in that hall that there was a disco every month or so.

We looked forward to those discos and they got very popular. The numbers of attendees swelled on disco nights, as the Aldenham opened its doors to other youth clubs in the area. In particular, there was a youth club in Highbury and when they came over there was a massive tear-up between their boys and the Aldenham boys.

Chris Foreman: Lee, Mike and me all lived close to the Aldenham. There were other youth clubs that we went to but it was the nearest. It cost something like sixpence to get in. It was a good place to chat up birds and get into shenanigans. It would be Lee, Mike and me, and Paul Catlin and John Jones, we were like a little gang.

We'd go to places like Parliament Hill Fields and set all the rubbish bins alight. We were over there one time and we could hear all these voices in the distance. It sounded like another gang. It was foggy but we all met up and got talking. They came from the Gospel Oak area – one of them was Tony Hilton. Our gang kind of amalgamated with theirs and this was the beginning of the Aldenham Youth Club mob.

The Aldenham was run by a nice couple, manager Mike, who was a big fat guy, and his wife. Mike was always smoking a cigar. But we used to just trash the Aldenham.

There was a big sports hall there that was like a 1950s bar. We'd spend a lot of time in there and it's where some of us met our girlfriends – I met my first wife there.

There was a dance held at the Aldenham every Friday. It was a disco, but it was just like those American movies where the boys would be on one side and the girls on the other. There was a guy called 'Elton P.', I think he thought he looked like Elton John – he wore big round glasses and he was a bit bald. He was the DJ on those Friday nights.

The Aldenham was our place but then some kids started coming down from Highbury. I think I tripped one of them up one night and the next week there was a bit more pushing and shoving. In the end it got to a point when there'd be battles every week.

I left the Aldenham on one of those nights and there were all these police waiting outside. They wanted trouble, so they got out of their vans and started bashing people. It wasn't even that anyone was doing anything, but the police had to be seen to do something. They arrested some people, threw them in the vans and took them down to the police station.

I remember Mike Barson and me put posters up saying things like 'Jimmy Savile will be coming to the Aldenham.' Mike, who ran the place, was pulling his hair out and taking the posters down. There was a kid who let off all the fire extinguishers, but Mike Barson got the blame for it and got banned from the club. It was really sad because we'd all go to the Aldenham and Mike would be sat on the wall outside. It was me who went to Mike [the manager] and told him that Mike [Barson] didn't do it. But I couldn't tell him who had really done it, because no way would you grass. Eventually Mike was allowed back into the club.

Mike the manager wanted to keep a tidy ship. I took it upon myself to put matchsticks in the valves of his tyres, as he'd banned a few of my mates. He saw me and chased me for quite a stretch; he was a rather big fella but out of condition, so I could outrun him. But when I got home he was talking to my mum – and rightly so, he was a real old-school bloke who'd shown a lot of patience.

There were a few hard-nuts at the Aldenham who were always getting into fights. Luckily, I was able to avoid any of the incidents. One such happened in West End Lane, where some friends got seriously attacked and hospitalised; another kicked off in Kentish Town, where Roy 'the Boy' Grimshaw received a headwound from a machete and his friend Dino was hit by a double-decker bus in the running battle. Suspects were supposedly identified as the Highbury gang.

The Highbury boys were testing us because we were getting a reputation as being a bit tasty. Rival youth clubs, like rival schools, were always at it back in those days. During one of those fights, I witnessed Mike Barson taking a strong punch on the side of his face that came out of nowhere, totally unprovoked. I think he'd been singled out because he was the tallest: take the biggest lad out first and the others will shit themselves and leg it.

It was a kind of ballroom blitz, creating a bit of panic, but the Aldenham stood their ground and saw the intruders off. It was after the machete incident that the away team stayed away, thank God.

Chalky: The first time I met Lee was around his flat in Denyer House. I'd only been there a few minutes and he tried selling me a box of batteries. He had a load of these AA batteries – this was in the days when no one needed lots of AAs because no one had the gadgets to put them in. He had something like a hundred and forty boxes and he was trying to get me to buy a job lot. It must have run in the family because the first time I met Lee's dad, he tried to sell me a car.

A load of us would meet up in pubs in Hampstead. Lee used to wear a lovely sheepskin coat that I really admired. We'd get to hear about parties happening in the area and we'd plan how to get into them. We always had to gate-crash because no one would actually invite us. Once inside the party we had a code word, which was 'mingle', and we'd blag it by saying we knew Sue or Sally. We'd also plan it so that we went in dribs and drabs, twos and threes, and once inside we'd filter off and eventually meet in the kitchen, diving into their alcohol. We'd often end up taking over these posh people's houses in Hampstead, taking charge of the record player and the drinks cabinet.

Because one of my uncles worked down Petticoat Lane, he bought material that my mum used to make shopping bags since the early 70s. She would make up to fifteen bags a day, which my uncle then sold on his market stall, bringing in a few quid for us.

It was my job to carry the fifty or sixty shopping bags. But I had to get them to my uncle, which meant jumping the train from Luton to Kentish Town. There were always people calling out to me, "Going shopping, Thommo?" This was at the time I was living in Luton and I hated it, so dropping the bags off to London was one of my ways of getting out of there. I had no friends in Luton, all of mine were back in NW5.

Luton had nothing to offer me. In fact I made enemies and had a few tear-ups with local lads, one of which blew up and resulted in me having to bring some of the Aldenham boys up from London to sort it out. Rob Bennet was built like a bear; Paul Catlin could outrun any sprinter; Den Pepper, Alan 'the Colonel' Hughes, Paul Chillo, John Bailey,

Bill and Pete Kennedy would just bog the opposition out; Gary Wootton was as mad as a box of frogs – he just had to bark and you'd run for the hills.

Pete McGee and Pat McCarney were the wild cards in the pack: they would merely spectate until things did get out of order, then strike a pose, give it a bit of the Kung Fu stance. Bruce Lee had broken box-office records and Carl Douglas was then on *Top Of The Pops* with 'Kung Fu Fighting'. When you shouted out to the Aldenham Glamour Boys, McCarney and McGee echoed up and down the M1 like a thunderous, two-headed beast.

There were a few characters from the Aldenham that went on to bigger and nastier things. There was one boy we called 'Heads', which was his graffiti tag, who was known for his one-punch knock-out. If you were unfortunate enough to be on the wrong end of his right uppercut, you weren't getting back up anytime soon. Lights out!

He was Highbury's most feared. I was always wary of being around him and careful of what I'd say. He was one person I didn't intend to get on the wrong side of. I already had a loosened tooth from a lad that went to Sir William Collins, the all-boys secondary school that taught boxing. If you got detention at that school, you had to stay and get in the boxing ring with other detainees. It deterred some pupils from getting into detention; for others, it was an honour to get in the ring and pummel their opponents.

Chalky: Lee was part of the Aldenham mob and they were quite well known. At the time I was knocking about with Suggsy and we were very aware of the Aldenham

94

boys' reputations. Some of the smaller groups, like Suggs and me and Lee and Chris, ended up joining to create a separate group. This was quite a while before the band got going. By the time of Madness we were already all firm mates. I think that was what made it. We became a group because we didn't really fit in anywhere else. We were like our own tribe. There was something quirky about all of us.

The Duke of Hamilton pub in Hampstead had a well-stocked jukebox in the basement. It was a focal point where we'd socialise at weekends in search of a *PARTY!* One evening after a rehearsal, some of The Invaders (the name we were trading under) would discuss all things musical past and present, how we were going to present ourselves, what direction we were going in, which record companies to approach. All this before we'd even cut our teeth – it wasn't a case of *if* but *when!!!*

Glam was being shown the door. Bowie fell to earth from the mesosphere to somewhere in LA – to carry on flying, high as a kite, to great success. Bryan Ferry moved into a less experimental arena after Roxy's fifth album, *Siren*.

I was very drawn to 1950s rock'n'roll and black R&B at this time – they were very 'in' around 1974/5. When 1950s America bopped back into vogue for the first time in twenty years, I welcomed the whole package with open arms. Elvis, James Dean and Marilyn were back in the party. The Screen on the Green cinema in Islington was showing 50s-set teen dramas like *The Lords Of Flatbush* and *American Graffiti*.

And, of course, *Happy Days*, with dropout heartthrob Fonzie, hit the TV screens with perfect timing – Friday teatime, as we chomped at the bit to get (in the words of 50s American covers group Sha Na Na) 'greased and ready to kick ass!'

If we were lucky, Bazooka Joe, a 50s-inspired band, would be performing at the town hall. Mike's brother, the drop-your-drawers-gorgeous Dan Barson, fronted the band with the yet-to-be-discovered pirate punkster Stuart Goddard (Adam Ant) on bass. Otherwise, entering the pubs around Hampstead, we'd discreetly seek out who was having a party at their parents' massive house…

As our interest in pubs, clubs and live bands grew, Mike, Chris and me took up arms. We'd outgrown the Aldenham Glamour Boys – now we had to find our own place in the world.

4

My Girl

It was whilst bouncing around the various youth clubs in the area that I started to see Debbie again. It was a few years on now since we'd first met at school in 1969. There was a period when I hadn't seen much of her due having to leave Acland and go to different places of education – and reformation.

It was at the youth club that I saw Debbie again. She had her own group who hung around Holloway Flats and they'd venture down to the Aldenham. I liked Debbie because she was a bit of a tomboy by nature. She liked to knock about with the local boys, could handle a bit of rough and even looked after herself when she went to watch the Arsenal on Saturdays.

The terraces were tough places in the 70s. One Saturday in the women's toilet, she was picked on by a few girls that looked as intimidating as they sounded. Deb just focused on one and knew what she had to do: *wallop!* Tufts of hair and ripped Brutus jeans. Deb's friend, Anne Harty, took it worse – she had her head banged against the toilet sink, which broke.*

When Deb and I saw one another again, we made a connection. There was a dancehall called Blackfriars in Queens Crescent, which played Philly soul, funk and some glam. It was a good place to be seen and to watch who was about. The girls would dance in small clusters and the boys would lean against walls with one leg up. There was a lot of posing and posturing, trying to look cool – as one does.

It was on one of those nights that we started to get together. I remember Debbie wore a beret over her permed hair, long before Kevin Keegan. I wasn't too sure about it at all. She was also into wearing lots of layers and unearthly shoes which, like most women, she seems to have an obsession with. (The quantity, not the style.) This has always been her thing. Her dress code is very individual.

We left the disco together and we knew then that we were attracted to each other. We chatted on the way back to her flats and when we arrived, I asked her out. It was January 6, 1975. We later had one of those silver coins embossed at the seaside, by an industrial metal-stamping contraption: it read, 'Lee and Debbie 06/01/75 to ????????.' She straightened her hair out soon after – no pressure from me though!

We started seeing one another and it lasted for about six months, then we broke up. It was all me really. I just

---

* I only went to the Arsenal twice – once with my son, who left the ground swearing and cursing and letting off steam. He was five at the time!

had a clash of feelings: commitment, responsibility, even claustrophobia.

However, after a two-week break I was so down about it that I went back to her, begging her to take me back. Thankfully, she did and we continued as boyfriend and girlfriend. I was at a loss during those two weeks, properly torn up. I hadn't experienced anything like it. It really hurt. I hadn't realised how much she made the butterflies in my stomach flutter.

I knew then that Debbie was special. There were lots of things that attracted me to her. She was one of the boys, very level-headed, a smart thinker – all those things that I wasn't – and I liked that. I was always mindful not to wear my loafers around her, after she'd done the tassels on my old ones – but it was okay, as by '75 I was more into wearing Dr Marten boots, soon to be painted in greens, blues and silver.

Debbie and I knocked about everywhere together. On a few occasions, I even tried to get her to come along and jump freight trains with me, but she wasn't having any of that. Although she was one of the boys, there were certain things she wasn't going to entertain. At those times I'd go off with my mates – Chris and Mike, Paul and Simon – and she'd hang around the jukebox at the Aldenham.

One of the things I believe she liked about me was that I didn't do the normal things most of the boys at the youth club liked to do. I think she saw me as having something different to them – and, of course, I had a half-decent mug and physique!

In those early days of our relationship we had an agreement. We would see each other most nights of the week, but on Friday nights I could see the lads. This seemed to work for both of us, even during the period when I needed to live in Luton.

I ended up living at Debbie's with her mum, Pam, and her dad, John. The first night was after I got a bit drunk and my mates took me back there. Pam and John were out playing darts down The Albion, their local. I was in Debbie's bedroom and I climbed into her bed. She chatted. I slurred and we had a cuddle. About 11.30, Debbie turned out the light.

She didn't seem concerned that I was in her bed and assured me that her parents never entered her bedroom. That was enough for me to feel I wasn't going to get sparked out by John, who had been in the army, laid glass paving lights that you saw outside shops in the West End and was a top painter and decorator – white-stained bib and brace overalls, but with work boots you could see your face in.

The light had only been off for a few minutes when suddenly the bedroom door burst open and Pam came charging in. "Debbie, you ain't going to believe it!" she cried. "I've won the set, 320. I was really on form tonight!" It was clear that she'd had a few gin and tonics.

While Pam was carrying on about the darts, I was trying to lie as flat and as still as I possibly could. Debs was trying to spread herself out across the bed. Pam finished what she had to share and, without suspecting anything, left the room and closed the door behind her.

I let out a huge sigh of relief and wiped the sweat off my forehead. I was just about to come up for air when the door opened again and this time it was John. "Debbie," he began, "you are not going to believe it!" and he started telling her about Pam's victory in the darts match. "Bullseye! Bullseye! Bullseye!" he kept shouting out as I was trying to keep still.

John eventually staggered out of the bedroom and I sheepishly came up gagging for air. It was a close shave but we got away with it. I don't know if John and Pam ever found out, but it was fortunate that we all got on.

I think John and Pam liked having me around because I kept things clean and tidy. I did my fair share of chores and making the tea too. Pam used to tell me she always knew when I'd made a pot of tea, because the kettle handle and everything else I touched was always to the left. I was the only left-handed person in the house.

I think Pam welcomed my domestic habits because she had four sons – Mark, Michael, Leigh and Darren – who didn't always tidy up after themselves, but took great care with their hair and appearance. Elder brother Mark had a naturally-tinted blond perm, which I forgave him for and tried to ignore, but he was one good-looking motherfucker. The brothers had appetites too, but whenever they left something on their plates I'd be straight in there, mopping up the leftovers. They thought it was disgusting, but I was a growing lad.

I got on well with all of Debbie's family. They were old-school working-class people and we understood each other. There were many times when I'd go for a drink with John and his lads. They treated me like a family member and I look back on that period with fondness.

Living at Debbie's was more laidback than living with my own parents, and especially Uncle Jack – who was a more regimented 'hands off cocks, on socks!' type of man. Although he used to keep me in line, we were a generation apart. He was set in his ways, loved his brandy and pub culture, worked hard and played harder, but we all loved him, including my mates. Debbie adored Jack.

Just as John and Pam and their sons accepted me, my family accepted Debbie. Even though there were chunks of time when my dad wasn't around, he did get to know her and they got on very well. Both families got along and this has remained so for forty-five years.

John and Pam developed enough trust in us to allow me to sleep in Debbie's room. Her bedroom was located on the third floor. There was a lamppost outside her brothers' bedroom window and (prior to being 'officially' allowed to stay over) I climbed up it several times to get in. It was like a farm in there at night – lots of smells and barnyard noises. All the brothers had to share a bedroom, so you can imagine it!

Pete McGee: Lee was the mountain climbing expert. He was able to get up a forty-foot drainpipe in about twenty seconds. He could be like a rat up the drainpipe. Even back then, he was a bit of an exhibitionist and loved to have people watch him whilst he climbed up things and tried to get into windows.

There was one occasion when I climbed up the lamppost only to discover that Debs' brothers' window was shut. I slid back down and went around to the other side of the house, where there was a balcony. Via that you could reach a small window that got you into the bathroom. It was just big enough for someone of my size and stature to squeeze through.

As I got in, I knocked over some toiletries and in the still of the night it made a fair racket. I next heard a door creak so I stood in a corner of the bathroom, as still and as a quiet as I could. It was pitch black in there. To this day I don't know who it was because I shut my eyes tight. They must have been thinking, 'Cheeky little bastard!' I waited in the bathroom for a further ten minutes before creeping back into Debbie's bedroom and jumping into bed.

I lived at Debbie's on and off for around two years – mixed in with also living at Uncle Jack's and in Luton. I lived like that until I got my council flat on the Caledonian Road in 1978. It was a fun time, carefree, and I'd met the woman I'd go on to marry and have children with.

I'd left school in April 1974. Family aside, the people in my life from that point were Debbie, Chris, Mike, Si Birdsall, Tony Hilton and a few mates from the Aldenham. Bobby Townshend had now gone down another route, soon to lose touch completely.

We were teenagers at a time when experimenting with things was a rite of passage. Alcohol and drugs were included in this – 'Bob Hope', 'griff', 'puff' or whatever we called it back then was fairly popular. I suppose it wasn't seen as anything too serious. Acid was floating about but it was probably more in fashion in the late 60s. Some of the kids at the youth club tried it a few times, but it wasn't really my thing and Chrissy Boy was quite anti-drugs. I remember rolling a joint one time when I was with Chris. I pigged out on it and was horribly sick. I had a proper whitey.

Chris Foreman: I didn't really smoke hash, Lee didn't either but somehow he had some. He thought it would be a good idea to roll a spliff outside the Houses of Parliament on a grassy area. Lee had a bit of a white-out and then the police came over; he was on grass and I had to get him off of the grass.

We ended up on the patch of grass outside Big Ben. We'd been on the bus, but because I felt ill we jumped off and I violently chucked up. I vaguely recall lying on the grass, with Big Ben's bells bonging, and looking up to see two coppers staring down at me. I'd had a slight accident and was messy. The police just told Chris to get me off because it looked like I was going to chuck up again, which wouldn't be good for the tourists to see.

I think that experience turned me off resin, so I never dabbled again – or I certainly never hogged the joint! I did have a soft spot for ganja – giggly gear – and my mate Pete McGee got me a microdot later on. Deb and myself were just retiring for the night and I was restless, went to listen to some of Ian Dury's LP *New Boots And Panties!!* and popped it in the Walkman. Other than my radiator doing a belly dance, my carpet turning into the Grand Canyon and my face melting downwards in the mirror, it was fine.

I needed fresh air and open spaces, so I headed toward Parliament Hill Fields (aka London's lung) pulled on some Levi's that felt like a sausage skin, got my tobacco, headphones and cassette player, then headed up toward Highgate West Hill.

No sooner was I trucking with my *New Boots And Panties!!* than a vehicle slowed up beside me. I casually put my hands in my pocket and kept walking, but when eventually I did look, I saw a vanload of Special Patrol Group. Thatcher had recently cobbled them together for stopping and searching, but they resembled a bunch of burly bailiffs to me. Fortunately, they drove on as, when I took my hands out my pockets, I had a lipstick in one hand and a tampon in the other. I'd obviously put my girlfriend's jeans on. Praise the Lord!*

*   *   *

Back in the mid-70s, I was reaching that age where I wanted to go and see live music in a pub and club atmosphere. This was the period when we went from groups like Mott The Hoople and artists like Bowie to watching the pub-rock groups like Dr Feelgood, Kilburn and the High Roads, Bees Make Honey, Ducks Deluxe and Eddie and the Hot Rods.

The pub-rock thing found homes in north London like the Hope & Anchor, the Lord Nelson, the Torrington Arms and the Sir George Robey. There was a strong connection

---

* I did discover magic mushrooms a few years later. I didn't mind taking them because you could gauge it more accurately than dropping an acid tab and waiting for the trip to happen. It was around 1991, just before the second coming of Madness at Madstock, I was having some good fun with mushrooms. But again, inevitably, I pigged. This time though it was half-purposely, venturing into another motherfucker, shitter-bugger dimension. I was very, very close to the edge of Syd Barrett fuck-off territory. But that is another episode, man, for another time…

with Essex too: the Admiral Jellicoe in Canvey Island had Dr Feelgood and Lew Lewis; the Kursaal Flyers were next door in Southend. All were Essex's secret weapons, rocked, cocked and two smoking tankards.

Back then we had so many options; we could go and see a group pretty much any night of the week. I remember seeing Dr Feelgood at Dingwalls before they got big, and then they were suddenly playing at Hammersmith Odeon where Chrissy Boy and I went to see them.

They had some good singles, like 'Back In The Night' and 'Roxette', and they looked brilliant on stage. They were intense live and watching Wilko Johnson and Lee Brilleaux left you sweaty and exhausted. They were like a couple of cherry bombs going off.

There were other performers who came out of pub rock, like Nick Lowe (from the band Brinsley Schwarz), Wreckless Eric and Elvis Costello (from the band Flip City). They had a unique sound that drew on traditional rock'n'roll and R&B. Pub rock seemed very much to me like our thing, it was all happening on our doorstep.

There was a lot happening in London, especially in the Camden area: I saw Kilburn and the High Roads at the Hope & Anchor, Dingwalls and the Lord Nelson, Holloway Road.

The first pub-rock gig of theirs I went to was at the Tally Ho, on the Fortress Road in Kentish Town. The Kilburns were Ian Dury's first band, which he formed in 1970. They were together for a few years but only released a couple of singles, 'Rough Kids' and 'Crippled With Nerves', and one album, *Handsome*.

Pete McGee: There were loads of bands playing but Ian's was our favourite. Ian with the High Roads had a really unique style that we took to. I think seeing Ian and his band influenced Lee a lot.

The Tally Ho was an old Victorian pub, typical of the kind of venue the pub-rock scene spilled out from. I wasn't old enough to legally buy a drink and shouldn't really have been in a pub without my parents. But back then you could get into pubs if you looked and acted old enough. There was no having to prove your age. It was Mike who used to go to the bar though, because he looked more adult and confident (and of course we paid him!).

I loved the sound that the Kilburns made, so seeing them live was a must. On that night at the Tally Ho, I decided not to go through the pub's front door – I don't know why, it wasn't even that you had to pay an admission fee. But I found a window at the side of the pub. (Several years later, when I saw it again, I couldn't believe I'd actually managed to squeeze through it – it was so small, like an oblong cat-flap.)

As I climbed through the window, some coins and a door-key I had in my pocket fell out. Looking down, I saw them lying in a puddle of water. As I was hanging from the window, some fella wandered in. I heard the clanging of metal before I saw the man.

When I looked round, a geezer with a croaky voice said, "What you doin' in 'ere?"

"I've come to see the band play," I replied.

"Well you won't fuckin' see 'em in 'ere, will you?"*

A bald boxer-type fella unhooked me. This, I was to learn later, was one Fred 'Spider' Rowe, Ian's minder by day and cat burglar by night (or so rumour had it).

I gave it a couple of seconds before making my way into the smoke-filled pub, which had attracted a very eclectic bunch of... I dunno, really. I felt like I could have babysat a few local old-timers by the time last orders rang out.

I was absolutely absorbed by the Kilburns' performance from the second they strolled on to the moment they

---

* It was a couple of years after first meeting Ian Dury at the back of the Tally Ho that I met him again. This time I was with Madness and we were on our way to the Pink Pop Festival in Holland, sharing a coach with Ian who by this time was with the Blockheads. I was sitting on my own when I looked up to see him approaching an empty seat beside me. He started up a conversation but it was weird: something along the lines of "See that fella out the window riding on that camel in the desert?"

He continued in this vein while I just nodded, thinking 'What the fuck is he going on about?' I didn't know if it was his art-school banter coming out or he'd indulged in a jazz Woodbine. I did start to feel a bit uncomfortable. The Madness sound-man at the time, Ian Horn, must have clocked what was happening and came over. But before he could say anything, Ian told him, "Just fuck off."

Ian Horn was only looking out for me because he knew Ian Dury could be a wind-up. Over time I learned this but my early encounters could be challenging, to say the least. We did become friends, though.

Ian also suffered his fair share of wind-ups. There's a story of how the Blockheads would take him back to his hotel room if he'd had too many drinks and dump in his bedroom. But to stop him going to the bar, they'd remove his leg irons. They just wanted to have a drink without Ian causing a punch-up. He had a reputation for causing trouble. There's another story of how Ian turned up at a casino and spotted Omar Sharif, who had two stunning girls sat either side of him. Ian went over to him and said, "How much for your women?" Omar responded by decking him. Looking down over Ian, he said, "They are my daughters."

awkwardly limped off – which sometimes could catch you by surprise, especially if front-man Ian lost his balance and fell over. Their drummer was a cripple on crutches and so was half-protected by his drum kit. They were theatrically quirky and their smutty sound went hand in glove with their smutty themes. Check out 'You're More Than Fair'...

When I watched the various pub rockers, I did feel an overwhelming desire to be in a group. If Andy Mackay of Roxy Music had just landed on our screens from Planet Spangle, sax player Davey Payne was an awesome inspiration you could not divert your eyes from: he'd pull something from his pocket that would spring up, light up or spin round, and sometimes the bell of his sax would start bellowing out thick smoke! He was the saxophonist in Kilburn and the High Roads – and, later, Ian Dury and the Blockheads.

Whenever I went to see the Kilburns, I made sure I secured a position directly in front of Davey. Ian was fantastic to watch too. Visually, they were just stunning. They were very music hall, mixing comedy with song and dance. It was something I connected with and would find its way into aspects of Madness.

Mike Barson: By the time of the pub-rock scene we were getting to see lots of bands, often. There was a period of time when being a musician had to be a really professional thing, as the bands played in huge venues, but then pub rock came along and changed all that. Pub rock was more like a bunch of amateurs telling us that anyone could do it. We liked that attitude and it showed us we could also be in a band. We watched how the bands did it. We'd go and see Alex Harvey, or Kilburn and the High Roads, and we liked the way they put on a show by being themselves. What they did felt real, it was like they were expressing themselves. It was often very theatrical and we took a lot of this sort of thing into Madness performances.

People like Ian Dury and Davey Payne were charismatic, they drew you in. They were about much more than just music, they were wacky and quirky. People must have loved them because the venues would always be well packed-out. The pub live gigs were £1 to £1.50 admission, or sometimes free. The breweries would give them a budget that the landlord would use to buy in entertainment. (This is still the case in many pubs with live music licences – up to £450 a month, so I've heard.)

Dave Robinson, who played a big role in the Madness story, also played a huge part in the birth of pub rock, showcasing many of the bands around town. I'd have probably rubbed shoulders with Dave at a Brinsley Schwarz gig but never knew it. This was in the days before he founded Stiff Records.

Back in 1975, there was also a group called Sore Throat. We'd go and see them quite a lot. They were from Highgate, right on our doorstep. They played a lot around the north London area and managed to get signed. 'I Dunno' was their debut single. They sort of fell in with the early punk and new-wave scene, and I liked the visual element Sore Throat had. They'd play their gigs all dressed the same, in velvet burgundy porter jackets.

Chris Foreman: There were two brothers in Sore Throat, Matthew and Danny Flowers, who I went to school with. We'd go and see them play a lot and one time I said to them, "We have this band, can we support you?" We supported them at the Moonlight Club, which was in West Hampstead, and again at the Music Machine. We had been called The Invaders, but Jimmy Pursey [of Sham 69] had a record label and signed a band with the same name. So we decided to call ourselves the North London Invaders – until Mike Barson said we should be called Morris and the Minors. That's what the poster for the Music Machine gig put us down as, but by the time we did that gig we'd come up with the name Madness. We played really good that night and I would say we blew Sore Throat off. After that they wouldn't give us any more support gigs.

There was a guy that Lee and me knew called Kevin Tame, he could play the guitar whereas I couldn't. Kevin and Carl Smyth [Chas Smash] jumped up on stage when we were playing and they started dancing. Kevin stayed for a bit before jumping off, but Carl stayed there and carried on dancing through the whole show. That was when he really started to become one of the band.

Before we were named Madness, we supported Sore Throat at the Music Machine. It was the biggest gig that we'd played to date. The Music Machine was an old Victorian Theatre opposite Mornington Crescent tube station, and would be one of the epicentres for punk.

The Invaders played ten to twelve gigs in schools, a college, a printer's works and a flower shop before naming themselves Madness. (But for most of these gigs, I was either not with the band or not there at all.)

Debbie: The group was using a dentist's to rehearse in and then they started to get enough songs together to get a residency at the Hope & Anchor, as well as the Dublin Castle in Camden. It seemed they got gigs in Liverpool and Manchester overnight. I don't recall them having an agent. Maybe John Hasler had contacts up north? Things were starting to move at pace for the band.

Pete McGee: I went to see Lee at the first gig he ever played. He was with most of the Madness line-up but they weren't calling themselves Madness at that time. I also saw them when they played their first gig at the Dublin Castle, and they were calling themselves Madness by then. We were all sitting around the pub and Lee was saying, "Come on, come and watch us!" He kept on at us, so we went down to see them play. At the end of the gig he came up to me and asked, "So what did you think?" I replied, "Fucking hell, Lee, it was a pile of shit!" I was only messing with him, but then I asked him how much he was getting paid. Lee told me that he was only getting two quid, so I offered to go and chin the geezer who was paying them.

Thankfully, Lee didn't take my comment too seriously and he stuck to playing. He knew that he couldn't really play the saxophone but, to his credit, he knew what he wanted to do and stayed with it. He taught himself how to play the instrument. Roxy Music and their sax player had a big influence on Lee. They really inspired him.

Roxy Music were very important to me. I had everything that they put out, up to *Manifesto*. I loved Bryan Ferry but it was Andy Mackay that had the biggest influence on me. It was because of Mackay that I wanted to play the saxophone.

Roxy were very space-age and visual, just like Bowie, so I was bound to connect with them. I saw them performing 'Virginia Plain' on *Top Of The Pops* in 1972: Mackay was wearing a glittery green shirt and yellow trousers as he blew into his saxophone. I was really impressed and knew that's what I wanted to do too. The B-side of the record was a track called 'The Numberer', an instrumental written by Mackay. It had a Kraftwerk feel but with a rasping sax throughout; with Brian Eno at the controls, it sounded unlike anything else around at that time – very adventurous.

As The Madness, Suggs, Chris, Carl and I would record a track called '4BF'. I wrote the song on an old piano that I bought and took home. It was all battered and buckled but I loved the character of it. The title was a direct reference to Bryan Ferry. There's even a lyric in the song that gives it away: 'Love was the drug that finally made you despair.' It has that typical Roxy fourth-album rhythm feel to it, especially the introduction. But my inspiration had come from Roxy's first album, a song called '2HB' that doffed the cap to Humphrey Bogart.

Even before discovering Roxy Music and Andy Mackay I had a clarinet, acquired from Haverstock School. I'd recently left the school and it was the Easter holidays. I went back with my cousin and my dad. Dad waited in a ticking car while I spanned the three-storey wall and slid open the window I'd unlatched months previously. Our double dustbin liners were then filled with instruments like trumpets, flutes and clarinets. (Trombones and French horns were too bulky.)

While I was making my exit down the school drainpipe, the flex that was tied to the top of the bags (which were in turn tied around me) started tightening around my neck. By the time I got to the ground I was seeing stars, due to oxygen starvation to the brain. I almost fucking fainted up there! There was a hangman's noose-like indentation that stayed for days. ('Cut here' sprang to mind.)

We loaded the bags into the boot and that was the last I saw of them. My dad went back to Great Yarmouth to try to flog them. He told me that when he took them into a shop, the shopkeeper quizzed him about where the instruments had come from; realising Dad's story was a load of cock and bull, the owner ended up chasing him out. But then, a couple of years later, I found out he'd sold them for a few hundred quid – the scoundrel! That hurt more than the noose.

I did manage to hold onto one of the clarinets, which went home with me. I tried to learn how to play it but it was really difficult to get any decent sounds out of it. The embouchure was taxing on the facial muscles and I pretty much gave up.

So I took it down to a shop at Dingwalls Market in Camden. There was a saxophone there that caught my eye – it turned out to be a Boosey and Hawkes tenor sax. It was in a horrendous condition but I liked it and I wanted it. I did a straight swap with the clarinet.

I now had my first saxophone. I got hold of a new ebonite-type mouthpiece and a few reeds (Rico 1.5 strength), and set about trying to learn how to play it. I only had that sax for a few months when I was approached by a pal from the Aldenham, 'Hotwire' Huesie, who acquired a new car every weekend and now had a saxophone. Someone he knew had climbed through a shop window on the Tottenham Court Road and stolen it.

Huesie knew I was learning to play so I was first port of call, but it was actually my girlfriend Debbie who paid for it. She gave it to me as a birthday present for my eighteenth. It turned out to be a Mark 6 Selmer, which is really sought after and worth a lot of money. I think Debbie paid £100 for that saxophone and I've still got it – my second love.

Pete McGee: A few of us were on our way back from the Sundown nightclub, which was on the Tottenham Court Road. We passed a brass-instrument shop and one of our group climbed onto someone's shoulders and managed to get through a window. Just as he got inside, the Old Bill came up the road – so we started to walk off, trying to act all casual and normal.

Our mate inside saw what was happening, grabbed an instrument and stood as still as he could, pretending to be a dummy. It worked, because the Old Bill walked straight past the shop without noticing him. He managed to get away with a few items from the place that night.

There's a scene in *Take It Or Leave It* where I go to a lesson with that saxophone. The teacher studies the sax and says, "Hello, what's happened here, the number seems to have been scratched off?" Looking a bit nervous and shifty, I reply, "Oh yeah, when I bought it the number was already scratched off." I then dig myself into a hole as I try to explain that I got it off a mate, who had got it from a shop. It all gets a bit confusing and the teacher gives up. If the truth be told, it was me who tried to scratch the number off but I made a mess of it, as it was punched into the actual metal.

I did actually go and have some lessons: at first a brass class in Highbury, and then I started to see an elderly gentleman who lived in Holborn. He was a nice old fella, who made a good, strong cuppa with rich tea and milk maids. He was patient and helped me out in the most therapeutic surroundings. But I couldn't keep paying out for one-on-one lessons, so I ended up back at a student group.

At the Aldenham there was a basement with some basic musical equipment, a beaten-up old drum kit and amps. I could go down there, mess around and make a racket, initially without any distractions. Once I started to learn the sax, I took it down there a few times. It wasn't an ideal practice spot though, as people would often pop in for a chat and to watch me blow, which was somewhat embarrassing.

As a result, I ended up practising at a place called The Thanet in Queens Crescent, which was a good half-hour walk from my home. It was another youth club that was just as rough as the Aldenham, but with less of a reputation. The Thanet had rooms where I could hide away and be left alone. My friend Eddie Joseph, who was a regular there and later became a youth worker, saw to this. That's what I needed to do if I was going to progress with the sax.

Tracy: I remember Lee showing up with a saxophone and thinking to myself, 'Why has he got that? He can't play it.' He was terrible at first, but he kept at it and gave it a good go. He'd practise at home but my mum couldn't put up with it, so she slung him out into a field at the back of our house.

Over time he got better and I could see him starting to take it more seriously. He went for a few lessons but because Lee was left-handed, the teacher couldn't help him. Because of this he basically taught himself how to play.

When the band started to rehearse more, I noticed Lee immersing himself in his music, in what the group were trying to do and to become. His saxophone playing improved seemingly overnight. He wasn't bad and he wasn't good, but he kept on trying. But I remember Brian Travers, from UB40, later saying to me that he felt Lee was one of the better sax players around at the time.

I didn't keep up with those lessons, but when I lived in Luton I started to dedicate more time to learning to play the sax. I spent hours playing along to records: 50s R&B, rock'n'roll, King Curtis, The Coasters, soul, reggae and, of course, Roxy Music – I imagined I was Andy Mackay.

Having the Selmer was like going from having a rusty old banger to a Rolls-Royce. My confidence grew and I felt increasingly encouraged to learn to play the instrument. I also changed the mouthpiece I was using and this helped improve my tone, if not my playing.

I was learning all the time, listening to recorded music with saxophones and/or brass sections. I was teaching myself and it took time. I didn't even learn how to tune a saxophone until after recording the *One Step Beyond...* album. My sax on the album is out of tune because I didn't know it needed to be tuned. But I like to think it was the sound of the sax that gave the overall Madness sound something unique, or 'nutty' – or maybe it just gave our producers an earache.

At the time, not even Clive Langer, who produced the album, said anything about the sax being out of tune. Maybe he didn't know either, but he'd work really hard with me in the studio to ensure I got it laid down just right. I'd be really nervous when it was my turn to be recorded and I know it held the band up. The truth was that I still didn't really know how to play. By the time Madness went into the studio, I think it had only been about two, maybe three years since I'd got my first saxophone.

It wasn't always easy finding the time to learn. I was still living at either Debbie's or in Luton. It was only when the band started to get serious about rehearsals that I got more serious about practising.

There was a massive field behind the house in Stopsley and I'd take myself out there with my sax tucked under my arm, a cassette player and a packed lunch. I'd then spend hours blowing into the sax and learning about minims, crotchets and quavers, practising scales and lengths of notes.

Debbie: Mike was the only one who had any musical training. He'd been learning to play the piano, and that part in *Take It Or Leave It* when he's trying to teach Lee and the others how to play is true.

I think it was Mike's brother who pointed out to us that my sax was in a different key to the other instruments. I didn't know that a tenor is in a different key to the alto and the alto is in a different key to the baritone. I had no idea that a concert 'C' on the piano is a 'D' on the saxophone, i.e. one tone higher.

As time went by I got better at playing the sax. Mike was already playing the piano and Chris started to learn to play the guitar. It was me that basically talked Chrissy Boy into buying a guitar. I took him down to a shop in Pratt Street, Camden. I'd been in the shop previously and adjusted the price tag, which was how we managed to get Chris his guitar at an affordable price.

He didn't really want to spend too much money because he was married and had his son by that time. He couldn't be seen to splash out hundreds of pounds on an instrument he couldn't even play. I think his wife ended up smashing that guitar to bits anyway; she definitely threw one out of the window, from the third floor.

Paul Catlin: At first Lee could only mess around with the saxophone, and then I saw him starting to get serious about playing it. When I'd go around to his, as I knocked on the door I'd hear him having a go up in his bedroom. As time went on, it started to sound better and better.

I thought it was great when Lee, Mike and Chris started to play together. Mike was already pretty good on the piano, and Chris and Lee sort of tried their best. The three of them had something. They were like the sun, the moon and the planets – they just worked. They became a unit and something grew between them as they became a band.

But there were times when Lee was out of the band for one reason or another, and I was there the night Mike rehearsed a new sax player. He was really good, but I caught him trying to nick some of Mike's records on his way out. He wasn't invited back.

Mike, Chris and me were a gang, and our gang was going to become a band. It all started to come together quite organically. We were best mates; we were going to watch bands playing live; we all loved music. Learning instruments and forming a band seemed like the natural thing to do.

We also looked at people playing in the pubs, when pub rock was happening in the mid-70s. And then punk bands were forming all over the place, performing in a variety of places. Like us, they could barely play a note. It fuelled us even more.

We were going to all the same venues that members of bands like The Clash and the Pistols were frequenting. A new live music venue in Camden with a late licence of 1am, Dingwalls, would attract young, angry, ambitious punks. I literally bumped into Steve Jones, coming out of the gents' one night. Some comment was exchanged, like, "Do ya get any fruit with that bowl?" ('Bowl' being a name for an aggressive walk.) If I replied at all, it would have been something like, "Have a banana!" (At least I managed to use the gents' loo, even if to piss in puddles.)

The Clash had their Rehearsal Rehearsals place in Camden, so they'd be about in places like Dingwalls and the Music Machine that had late licences. Motörhead's Lemmy was a regular too. It was a healthy mix of aspiring young oiks, in a period when anything seemed possible.

5

Living For KIX

If you walked around the areas of Highgate, Camden and Highbury from 1974–76, you couldn't fail to notice 'KIX 681', 'Chrissy Boy' and 'Mr B' written on the sides of buildings. These were Mike's, Chris's and my own tags. KIX was about 'living for kicks' and 681 was the number of the house I lived in back in Stopsley, Luton.

My interest in graffiti was sparked after seeing an article in the *Sunday Times* colour supplement. (I think Mike had seen it and shown Chrissy Boy and me.) We pored over the photographs and read about how graffiti was becoming very popular in the States, causing problems for the local authorities, so we thought we'd try it. It seemed risky, exciting, artistic – but it wasn't a statement about politics or social frustration. It was just us making our mark. We thought we might be able to do something that livened up the area up.

There was already a pretty good artistic streak between Mike, Chris and me, so graffiti was going to come easy to us. Plus we liked the thrill and adventure of getting up to whatever teenagers do. Mike was probably the better artist, but then he'd gone to art college for a while before dropping out to pursue other options – like doing his own thing and rock'n'roll.

Chris Foreman: There was a book that came out in 1974 called *Watching My Name Go By*, which was about graffiti in America. The *Sunday Times* wrote about it. After that we started writing graffiti. Mike and Lee were very prolific. Mike is incredibly artistic and the stuff he did was really good. I remember at Hampstead station he did this locomotive that looked like something from 1950s America. Lee used 'KIX 681' and wrote that everywhere. We graffitied all over our part of London. I stopped doing it when I met a girl and it all started to seem a bit childish to me.

We'd go to the local Woolworths to acquire our tools for the job in hand. They had a decent-sized section of different coloured spray cans. It's not as easy getting hold of spray cans these days, which I suspect is due to kids using them for graffiti. Cleaning it up probably puts a dent in councils' budgets.*

---

* My youngest son, Kye, has taken up graffiti and does his thing in places that are set up for kids to do just that. So he's not going off into areas of danger, like electric rail lines. It's a way of trying to control it and to reduce the amount that ends up on the streets, in areas where graffiti might be unsightly.

It was easy to exit Woolworths with a few spray cans. Then we'd go to explore Camden, Highgate and so on, looking for a canvas amongst the concrete to tag. It became a game of cat and mouse as we evaded the authorities.

Our aim was to find more unusual places and we tried, very hard, not to graffiti private residences. On one of our adventures we found a car near Hampstead Heath. It had been in an accident where it hit a bend too quickly, skidded and went flying through the air, rolling over a few times before landing back on its wheels. And that's where it remained, as the grass grew up around it. Mike, Chris and I set about spraying the car. Mike drew a really good hand that linked with his tag, 'Mr B'. It looked like blood was dripping from the fingernails, really impressive but creepy!

Another favourite piece of graffiti is actually still there: it has 'Dare Devil – DD', 'KIX' and 'Mr B' high up on a side of a building on my old playground, Tammo Land (now the Ingestre Road Estate). We managed to graffiti in an area three storeys up. It used to puzzle people how we'd managed to do it. What they didn't know was that we did it when some workmen put scaffolding up, climbed up there in the dark of night, did our graffiti and disappeared into the shadows.

One of our favourite places to tag was on the side of railway bridges. Just being in the vicinity of trains and railway tracks was a buzz. Quite a few times we left our tags on trains. Unlike the underground trains of today, back in the 70s they had a driver's compartment in the middle as well as at the front. The trains had sliding windows too, which we could open to spray our tag. When the train pulled away, people would have to glance again to see what we'd done so quickly on the far side of the rail lines.

It was a massive buzz to go out and do graffiti. Part of the thrill was identifying the most risky or unexpected places. Hanging off the side of bridges was always fun. It was awkward and dangerous, and that's why we liked doing it. It was probably fucking stupid too, because it meant being dangled over the side of the bridge whilst someone held onto your ankles. You'd be trying to leave your tag whilst catching glimpses of cars speeding below you.* (Today you hear of fatalities on railway property or areas of high risk – some poor kid gets electrocuted or hit by a train. I really would urge them not to take those risks.)

In the late 70s there were a lot of group names sprayed on walls – The Jam, The Specials, Madness – and, of course, football teams: Chelsea, Arsenal, West Ham. Or there would

---

* For years, there used to be graffiti written on the old Edwardian bridge that crosses M25 junctions 16–17: 'Give Peas A Chance.' That can't have been easy to do! Sadly, in 2018, someone replaced 'Peas' with 'Belch' – whatever the fuck that means. It really upset a lot of people. Such was the popularity of the original graffiti that a Facebook group was started with around ten thousand followers. It's been replaced recently yet again, with 'THANK YOU NHS'.

I used to see another piece of graffiti on a brick wall leading up to Archway Hill: 'Twitch for Sam Surfer.' I have no idea what that meant, but it's cool as. One that made me laugh said, 'I'm a hog for you Deirdre,' which I think a friend of ours called Mick had something to do with possibly. (It was taken from a Coasters song, 'I'm A Hog For You Baby'.) I'd also see some graffiti which said, 'I'd rather have a bottle in front of me than a frontal lobotomy,' which is priceless.

be political stuff like 'NF', 'Anarchy rules OK', 'George Davis Is Innocent'.*

Graffiti in the UK was different to what we saw in the USA. The Americans seemed to put a lot more into it, even though it was undecipherable. We'd see photographs or scenes in films of the subway trains covered in huge, brightly coloured tags and quotes. It was much more than just graffiti, it was art. Around London it was mostly quite basic: 'I was here', or, 'Fuck off', or just a drawing of a cock. But when you saw what those kids were doing on the streets of, say, New York, Detroit or Philadelphia, it was impressive.

I found a photograph recently that I sent to Suggs, because I knew he'd be impressed. It was of a clipping from the local rag, the *Hampstead and Highgate*, in 1975. It shows the tags of DD (Dare Devil), who was Simon Birdsall, and Seudo, who was John Hasler, at various times our drummer, manager or singer, Bilko, Heads (Bill Kennedy), KIX and Deb (plus a heart with an arrow going through it) and Mr B, who had written 'Kilburn and the High Roads'.

The tags were actually graffitied on the side of quite a posh house in Hampstead. I admit we shouldn't have done it and I did feel a bit bad about it. If the owners ever read this and it was your house in 1975 – well, you have our profound apologies.

---

* When I first moved to Barnet, on the edges of north London, someone had written 'NF' (National Front) on a wall, which I was disappointed to see. But then shortly after, someone changed the 'N' to 'No' and the 'F' to 'Future'. (That must have been inspired by the Sex Pistols song 'God Save The Queen' – maybe!)

The period when we were doing graffiti didn't last long, maybe eighteen months. It was part of that rite of passage and at the time it was fun. In the beginning it was quite basic and often quite naff, but by the time we hung up our spray cans what we were doing looked pretty good.

When you're young, time seems to go quicker – then, before you realise it, it's gone! A mere combination of moments, right?

I lived in a bubble and didn't really connect to what was going on outside of my world. It was the 1970s. There were strikes, political tensions, the IRA were very active and there were wars going on all around the world, but that stuff never really touched me. I was enjoying my life, soaking up the experiences and taking advantage of the opportunities the streets of London offered.

I have an abundance of good memories between the period of release from Chafford Approved School, in February 1973, and the band starting up. It was a very creative time. We made our own fashions, as I've mentioned, and I still own a pair of patchwork boots I had made opposite Zipper in Camden Lock. I wish I'd kept a pair of the DMs I painted and encased though. They could tell some stories...

We felt free, like we could come and go as we pleased. And we did!

True, there was the 'winter of discontent': the dustmen striking in 1978, which meant piles of rotting rubbish on the streets. Back in 1973 there were the blackouts, the three-day week when electricity was available for part of the day and the rest of the time there was darkness. I don't remember how long this period lasted – but I do recall having a field

127

day leading up to the season of good cheer, in the shops of the West End.

I'd be out with my mates most of the time, but when I went home to have my tea or a bath, I'd catch up on a bit of TV. I mainly liked to watch comedy. We had people like Benny Hill, Tommy Cooper, Spike Milligan and Dick Emery to cheer us up, and Dave Allen's sketches were inventive. I made time for comedy and the occasional *Professionals* or *Sweeney* episode, but family soaps like *Crossroads* and *Coronation Street* were never going to draw me in.

By the time I was seventeen, I was outside the family home more than I was in it. I saw more of people like Debbie, Mike and Chrissy Boy than I did my own family. I was at that age when you're not quite old enough to go to boozers but too old to continue to go to youth clubs, the transition period that all teenagers had to go through. I felt at a loose end, but I wasn't going to accept just sitting indoors all the time, vegetating in front of the TV.

Besides, getting up to mischief was much more fun. Mike, Chrissy Boy and I shared a lot of experiences together during this period.

I recall a time when Mike and I were strolling down the street, minding our own business. A police car pulled over and two coppers got out, to rifle through our pockets. They found a hip flask on Mike that had some whisky in it. We were underage, so they gave us a bollocking – and took our alcohol!

On the same night, Mike and I stumbled across a blues party. We were walking down a street and heard some reggae, coming from a house. We decided to check it out, so walked into a hallway that led up to some stairs. I went up the stairs and found the electricity meter; I also found a piece of metal that I used to break into it. (I knew it was loaded by the sound it made when you tapped it.)

Whilst I was trying to get into the meter, I heard a voice calling, "Lee, Lee, Lee, Lee!" I looked down and saw Mike. It must have been the position I was in, as well as being a bit pissed, but he looked very tall. He was also surrounded by a load of black people, who all looked like midgets.

I stopped what I was doing and legged it further up the stairs until I reached the skylight. I pushed it open, climbed up and suddenly found myself hanging onto the roof tiles.

In my attempt to escape, I left Mike behind – which was well out of order, really. But I couldn't get back to him. Instead, I found myself sliding down the tiles. As I did, I grabbed hold of the guttering and then a lead pipe. It cut my hands up, like a thousand fucking papercuts.

Once I reached the ground, I ran through some gardens and got torn up by some prickles on a bush. I ran down to the corner of the street and hid, scanning the area for Mike. I didn't see him again that night – although, funnily enough, it never came up in conversation.

Blues parties were popular in London with the working-class Caribbeans who'd come to live in the UK. They were basically parties held in someone's home. People turned up with the booze and ska and reggae records, and there would often be thick ganja smoke hanging heavily in the air. My sister used to go to a lot of blues parties.

*   *   *

From its opening in 1973 to 1983, Dingwalls was a magnet for clubbers, unknown and cult bands, music lovers and late-shift workers – like restaurant owner and semi-celebrity George Tilley, who, along with his mum, served up typically English dishes. His mum's chicken and mushroom pie was second to none. I asked him once, "How do you get your mash potato so creamy?" He replied, "I spunk in it!"

He was in a different class and on another planet. Prior to shutting shop and a swift three-minute walk to 'Dingo's', his night would start with a 'hot knife' inhaled with what resembled a small car exhaust-pipe, followed by a line of sulphate the length of a baby's arm, smoothly sunk with a large Rémy Martin, no ice. *Bosh!* I thought I was rock'n'roll, but he invented the bastard. We got on dangerously well. No wonder he's now dead.

We'd become very close friends, going on skiing holidays together. I'd best stop it there, but the French gendarmerie saved us from several close shaves over in Courchevel.

Our mate Alex Doolally brought a bottle of poppers to the packed Dingo's bar once; several of us had a deep pop. I thought McGee's head was going to explode – I know I felt mine was. Fuck that shit, it was radio rental*...

Dingo's was relaxed on underage drinking provided you were sensible. There were no lumps putting the pressure on you to 'get the fuck out'. Pubs back in the 1970s closed at 11pm and last orders would have rung out fifteen minutes before, with the landlord yelling, "Ain't you got no homes

* Rhyming slang!

to go to?" Unless you were in with the Arlington House group, you wouldn't have been aware of the loopholes for some of the local watering holes in Camden.

By the time Madness started playing live there was an established music circuit in and around Camden. It was lively, vibrant and healthy – unlike today, when so many pubs and venues have been closed down.

Although there was something to see any night of the week, there was still something special about the weekend. People worked Monday to Friday, there was less Saturday/Sunday working than there is today, so by the time Friday came people were ready to get their rocks off. This was often evident on a Saturday afternoon at the football terraces, which could be violent places – but then so could gigs, especially punk gatherings.

Pogoing could be disastrous, especially if someone jumped up as another was coming down. As for the spitting, drop me out. The Jam played the Nashville Rooms one time and there were green 'grollies' stringing through the airline. Some landed on Paul Weller, so he and his crew jumped into the crowd and Rickenbacker-ed the culprits.* Generally though, people just wanted to enjoy themselves and let rip.

There was a lot going on around this time. Punk was also about to crash-land in a London TV studio, stamping its mark on the nation and its media. Just as I was about to head out the door to London, after tapping my dad for a few

* Mr Barson had to bop an LA punter on the nose at the Whisky A Go Go due to this fad.

quid, I heard the Rolling Stones mentioned* – so I thought I'd take a gander.

It was a live primetime interview I'll never forget, a moment in time when you remember exactly where you were and what you were doing. Bill Grundy introduced our new heroes, the Sex Pistols. Rock'n'roll had returned after a twenty-year sabbatical, or incubation – with a vengeance! Only Grace Jones' live TV attack on Russell Harty, several years later, was as spectacular.

Its riotous shockwaves would ricochet off your primetime TV screens, shaking hapless presenter Grundy. A lot of new groups were discovered in the wake of the Pistols' sweary conversation – and Madness would be one of them, eventually.

Wannabe bands and upcoming chancers were most likely in the same music clubs and venues, all larging it at the same time unbeknownst to each other. Every wannabe would have loved to do what the Pistols did that night – but we didn't, did we? You were watching a mirror image of yourself in that TV interview, having an out-of-body experience.

I needed to get out of Luton so I decided I'd start squatting in London. I had some row with my parents over something silly like the telephone bill and it was a matter of, "Right, I'm off."

The first squat I used was on the Hampstead Road Estate. I was working for Camden council at the time as a painter

---

* "Not the nice, clean Rolling Stones – you see, they are as drunk as I am..." – Bill Grundy, introducing the Sex Pistols on the *Today* programme, December 1, 1976.

and decorator. One of my jobs was to decorate this flat on the top floor; the lift never worked so I was forever having to carry all my stuff up and down the stairs. I did a good job decorating the place, so I decided I'd just stay there. I went out and got bedding, cups and plates, all mainly pinched from Woolworths, and all the things I'd need to make it a liveable space.

I also changed the locks so that only I could get in. There were a lot of people squatting in London at the time. It was estimated that there were nearly thirty thousand of us in the late 70s. At St Agnes Place in Kensington, the entire street was made up of squatters. There was often conflict between the various councils and the Family Squatting Movement, plus a siege or two. I knew plenty of people that used squats: you could find one and move in, stay for a bit, move out and find another. It was pretty easy to do.

(Some squats were in better shape than others. I had friends who squatted down in King's Cross and they weren't the best I'd seen.)

One afternoon, I was carrying some of the stuff I'd acquired from Woolworths and the police stopped me. They asked me where I'd got it all from. I explained that Debbie and I had just got a flat and that's what the stuff in the bags was for. They wanted me to produce receipts, but of course I couldn't. I told them Debbie had sent me out with a list of items, so they asked me where they could find her.

They really went to town in an attempt to prove I'd stolen the stuff. They even turned up at the Queens Arms pub, where Debbie was with her parents. She recalls how the pub door opened, two police officers walked in and she knew immediately they were there for her.

They walked over to the bar and asked the barman to point out Debbie, then took her to one side and questioned her about the things I'd told them. They even asked her to describe some of the items I'd had in my bags. All she could do was fumble her way through a list of things like a toilet brush, cups and saucers, bedding and so on.

They had actually arrested me. I was waiting in the cells at Albany Street police station until they'd spoken with Debbie and felt satisfied the items had been paid for.

Out of all the places I squatted in, I only had one run in with the council – in the flat that I'd decorated. They came round and I had to let them in. They had a good look and basically told me it was one of the better squats they had come across. But as impressed as they were, they weren't going to allow me to live there, whether rent-free or not. I'd have to move out pronto.

I pleaded with them and put my case forward: I was homeless, single, had a job but couldn't get on the waiting list for a council place. It didn't work and I had to find somewhere else. (I did eventually get a council place on the Caledonian Road, where Debbie and I first started to live together as a couple.)

I went to another squat right next door to where Chrissy Boy was living prior to officially being housed. I probably went down to see him and noticed the place was empty, thinking it would make a nice home for me. I managed to break in and sweep to one side the piles of letters building up on the floor.

I turned it into my place and stayed there for several months. I moved out because, as much as I liked it, it ended up becoming a party place. On one occasion, our friend Tony Hilton threw up right next to Chrissy Boy's guitar, splattering it. This happened around summer, and the smell hung around for some time after. I can still half-taste the stench when I recall that squat.

I also had people turning up at any time of any given day, and it all got a bit too much for me. I'd had enough – it was time to vacate the premises.

6

Brand New Beat

By 1975, the pub-rock scene had been joined by the likes of The Stranglers and Joe Strummer's 101'ers. But that scene was about to be swept aside and replaced by something new – punk rock. This was an explosion that was still going to be felt decades after.

The pub-rock thing definitely opened the doors for bands that couldn't read music. It would play a huge part in the formation of Madness. But I was aware that something new was happening. I could feel that something was changing. Alongside the music, I started to notice it in the fashion. I was certainly curious about what people were starting to wear in the clubs and pubs.

By the time I caught wind of what was happening, the punk thing had already been going for a few months. But it wasn't like I was getting along to any of the gigs. Suggs was talking to me just the other day about the punk bands he'd go and see at places like the 100 Club and the Roxy. He was specifically telling me about Don Letts.

Now Don was the resident DJ at the club and played reggae and dub, possibly introducing a lot of punks to the music. The reason he played reggae was because, in 1976, there just weren't that many punk records available.

The Roxy opened in December 1976, in an old fruit and veg warehouse in Neal Street, Covent Garden. A guy called Andy Czezowski was behind it, who'd later start another punk club called the Vortex. The Roxy didn't stay open that long, but while it did groups like The Clash, The Damned, The Jam and The Police played there.

It also catapulted Don Letts into the punk limelight and he became close friends with The Clash. A photograph of him was even used on the cover of the *Black Market Clash* album, showing Don strolling towards the police line during the 1976 Notting Hill Carnival riot.

Don wasn't just a DJ though, also turning his hand to making films and documentaries. With a little help from his friends he'd finance *The Punk Rock Movie* in 1978, including his footage of the Sex Pistols, The Clash and Generation X.*

I didn't frequent those punk clubs that much. It just wasn't my scene really. I agreed with the message that punk was putting out, but in many ways I was just blinkered to it as my interests lay elsewhere. I was aware that what was going on in the clubs was fresh, it was moving forward and it was a UK export. I wasn't opposed to it at all – it just wasn't for me or my mates.

---

* In more recent years, Don Letts directed *Westway To The World*, the documentary film about The Clash. After punk, Don teamed up with Mick Jones from the band to form Big Audio Dynamite and they had some success with 'E=MC²'.

What Don Letts played absolutely appealed to me though, it was right up my street. The 1970s was a really good period for roots reggae. I saw Bob Marley perform 'Stir It Up' and 'Concrete Jungle' on *The Old Grey Whistle Test*, which was a revelation for me and a whole generation of people.

I think punk really hit home for me when the Sex Pistols appeared on the *Today* programme. Bill Grundy hosted that popular show at 6pm, when there were a lot of people sitting down in front of the telly having their tea.

Queen were due to be on the show but for some reason had to cancel. That's when the Sex Pistols crash-landed into the TV studios from the King's Road, to replace them. The group lounged across the sofa while some of the Bromley Contingent (Siouxsie Sioux was one of them) were interviewed by Grundy. It just went downhill from there as the Pistols tossed in a few 'fucks', 'shits' and 'bastards'.

Steve Jones called Grundy a "dirty bastard" and a "dirty fucker" after he'd invited Siouxsie to meet him after the show. In 1976, swearing on national TV was a big no-no.* The newspapers had a field day with headlines like 'The Filth And The Fury'. From out of nowhere, the Sex Pistols became household names and Bill Grundy's career went into decline.

I remember the whole thing as clear as day, all these years later. I recall feeling a bit sorry for Grundy too, but

---

* I read Steve Jones' book recently, *Lonely Boy: Tales From A Sex Pistol*, and I can understand why he said what he said that evening.

he was pressing them and goading them. Johnny Rotten and Steve Jones weren't going to pass up on that.

I was sitting down with my mum and dad at the time, thinking that any minute now my dad was going to throw his plate at the telly. But he was just intrigued. My mum was gobsmacked, not knowing where to look. My dad asked, "What have I just witnessed?" I replied, "This is not going away anytime soon!" Just like thousands of other teenagers, I thought what I'd just seen was fantastic. The old guard certainly got it stuck up them that night and many never recovered.

It wasn't that I didn't like punk, but the fashions weren't my cup of tea. I remember going to the Roxy, seeing what people were wearing – all that stuff from the SEX shop and bin liners – and thinking, 'No!' I bowled past. Of course, I'm gutted now as the place was so important to punk history.

I did Chageramas, but people were spitting all over the place – over the band members, over one another. That wasn't for me either. I never liked it when people did that at some of our early Madness gigs either.

Despite punk being the new kid on the block and people like Don Letts introducing reggae to the wider public, I felt that Roxy Music and Bowie were still making good records too. Plus I was kind of going backwards: listening to doowop, Motown and Stax, and the rhythm and blues that came out of America during the 1950s and 60s.

Chrissy Boy and Mike weren't overly into punk either. Chris was still listening to the heavier stuff and he much preferred the smaller, pub-type gigs, which more stimulating without the saliva.

Mike probably accepted the more intelligent punk, but he was more into Elvis Costello – he was a big fan of his music, his image, and he really liked keyboard player Steve Nieve's style. Mike did go to see the Sex Pistols down in the Nashville Rooms, when it was about 50p to get in, but then he was open to all sorts of music: anything from ska to Elton John, James Taylor and Neil Young.

What I did like about punk was the way it swept aside all that prog-rock stuff so forcefully. That wasn't a bad thing at all, because there were too many twenty-minute keyboard solos going around. I certainly went along with the punk attitude when it came to this.

But otherwise, the 1970s was a brilliant era for music. So much happened: from reggae and soul to glam and pub rock, from punk and new wave and then, towards the tail-end of the era, to the second mod and skinhead waves, and 2Tone. Madness would pull in a lot of the post-punk crowd, but we'd also appeal to the skinheads and mods.

In a funny kind of way, I actually like the punk groups more now than I did back then. I listened to the version of 'My Way' by Sid Vicious recently to remind myself how good it is, certainly the promotional clip. Anything by The Clash still sounds good too, but I did discover them mostly at a later date. This may have partly been because, at the time and when Madness were getting up and running, I saw them as another band we were competing with, which was a short-sighted attitude.

I saw The Clash as being similar to Madness – yeah and why not? We liked the same reggae style an' ting. The Clash were harder and more politically aware than us in their lyrics, but I remember Mark Bedford really liked them. (As did the other members of Madness, although one or two might not have said so at the time.)

Even one of our moves was borrowed from Mick Jones and Paul Simonon: the three-pronged attack, a dynamic, in-your-face stance where they moved in close either side of their vocalist, Strummer.* The Clash did their reggae stuff very well and I really liked Paul's bass playing. He played in a way that allowed the songs to breathe, nothing flash. I certainly felt that he'd practised along to his reggae. Equally important, he looked the part.**

---

* Chris and Mark seem to do that more these days, propping their hero up. Maybe I'll pull the plug on that lyric prompt one day!

** I've never met Paul Simonon in person but I've spoken to him over the phone. Neither Madness nor Crunch! (the band I started with Chris Foreman) were going at the time, so I was in the process of trying to put a ska band together. When I was thinking about a bassist, I thought of Paul. Sadly, this was at a time when he was busy with his art project and he just didn't have the time to commit. But I'd been keen on Paul being a member because he looked good, had a great image and played bass in the style that I liked. I didn't want a bassist with all the technical funk-ability, I wanted something more ska/rock steady.

Another person I approached about this new band was Johnny Marr. Johnny was sold on the idea but, like Paul, too busy at the time. (I think he was doing something with Crowded House.) I was very chuffed that both had been willing to talk with me about the band idea, it's just a shame that it never happened.

I liked Johnny's style of playing and had been a fan of the earlier stuff that he'd done in The Smiths – although I'm not a big fan of Morrissey. Morrissey's lyrics are depressingly evocative though, and it was very thoughtful of him to send me his album *Your Arsenal* with a scrawled message reading, 'Be Bold, Be Brave, Be A Man.' I thought, 'How about a kick in the backdoor?!' (It was just prior to Madness Madstock reunion and Chrissy Boy and me trying to launch our Nutty Boys band in the early 1990s.)

The Clash had Rehearsal Rehearsals at the Star Warehouse in Camden Town, but relocated in some place near the Westway when things got busier for them. It was very rough and ready. The area at the time was very derelict and abandoned – perfect for when the warehouse rave thing came along a few years later.

It's a pity that Madness and The Clash never really had much to do with each other. There is one story, however. Both bands were in the Westway/Shepherd's Bush area at the time Madness were filming the video for 'Shut Up'. We were dressed up as policemen and I had these big, clown-type shoes on. They were hard to walk in, let alone running or climbing steps.

During the making of the video, there'd be breaks where the crew would prepare for different scenes – like the piano falling from the sky. Someone must have heard that The Clash were nearby, as it was suggested that paying them a visit might be fun – especially dressed up as coppers.

I'm a lover of the music The Smiths made and Johnny Marr was a big part of that sound. I thought he would be a good addition to my ska band idea because I didn't want a strict reggae guitarist. The drummer I had in mind was John Bradbury – Mr Rimshot of The Specials. My back-up plan if John wasn't available was Charlie Charles of the Blockheads. With these guys in mind I pictured this post-punk supergroup, but it just never happened. I even had a couple of potential names: one was Kosh and the other was The Animist – animism being the belief that everything in the universe, whether animal or inanimate object, is alive. I probably wouldn't have stuck with that one because it was a bit 'Genesis', but in the end the band never came to fruition.

None of the songs I wrote for that band got used either. I still have them on cassette collecting dust somewhere. I might present them to Madness one day, who knows?

So, being a bit bored and feeling a bit mischievous, we burst into the room where The Clash were. The next thing we knew, they were caught in the headlights: rushing around, flushing stuff down the toilet, heading for the exit sign. In that moment they thought it was an actual police raid – it was vividly real, loud and authoritative.

I never actually got to see The Clash play live. I know some members of Madness did and one of those times was in New York City at a time when they were playing at Radio City. Members of both bands frequented the same clubs and pubs but, sadly, my path never crossed with theirs.

Like with The Clash, back in the punk days I didn't have much to do with The Jam either. But I did meet Paul Weller on a couple of occasions. The first was when Madness was staying at the Tropicana Motel in Los Angeles. It was one of those rock'n'roll hotels made famous by the bands that stayed there while on tour. Acts like The Doors, Tom Waits, Ramones and Blondie all passed through until it closed in the late 1980s, to make way for a huge Ramada hotel.

Madness finished their whirlwind ten-day tour of the US in sunny California. We didn't like doing long tours there, and anything over three weeks seemed too long. We missed our PG Tips and rainy weather, and wanted to be back home.

In amongst all the gigs and the travelling, Stiff arranged for us to have a couple of days off and booked us into LA's Motel Tropicana. They didn't hear any complaints from us. The sun was shining, the drinks flowed and we had a rock'n'roll party around the swimming pool that the motel rooms surrounded.

The rooms were basic, just like you see them in the films: a bed, a TV and a bathroom, with a shower curtain you expected Norman Bates to appear behind at any moment. The rock'n'rollers that stayed at the motel were able to get away with pretty much anything, so all kinds of behaviours and naughtiness went on in the rooms or around the pool.

I think it may have been our promoter who put the party on, or maybe it was just something that happened naturally when bands were at the motel. But it wasn't too long before a party was in full swing with band members, fans and groupies.

I remember most of the band felt knackered from all the gigs and travelling, but we were supplied with things that kept us propped up – like matchsticks and broomsticks. I had a pair of NHS glasses I'd adapted with mirror lenses on that tour – they first appeared in the 'Grey Day' video clip when I was playing that plastic sax, then when I was dressed as a cowboy complete with bowlegs.

I was wearing the glasses whilst talking to some Norman Bates guy around the pool, when for some reason he started to freak out. I recall him telling me that he could see right through me, so I don't know what type of medication he'd been handed. But I was clenching in all departments, readying myself.

He got more and more strange. I felt convinced that at any moment he'd pull a gun out. But I stood my ground and tried to disguise the fact that I was now starting to freak out, too. All I could hear in my head was Robert De Niro's voice repeating, 'You talkin' to me? *Are you talkin' to me?*' I put it down to drugs and Jack D., on top of sleep deprivation, on my part.

As I was listening to Norman and watching his hand movements, from the corner of my eye I saw a naked body leap into the air and jump into the swimming pool. At first I didn't think too much about it. There were bodies jumping in and out of the pool all of the time – maybe not all bollock-naked though.

I next noticed a few chairs getting launched into the pool too. Things were getting a bit rock'n'roll. I still had that American bloke banging on about how he could see through my noggin, but I used the pool incident to make my escape. I was also starting to think that whoever it was that jumped into the pool was taking their time coming up for air.

I edged my way nearer to the pool and, as I got closer, the naked body jumped back out. Paul Weller stood there, naked as the starry night itself, with his hands covering his meat & two. I couldn't believe my eyes. I mean what was the shy, unassuming, reclusive boy wonder from Woking doing dripping wet around the pool at the Tropicana?

Well, the story goes that for some reason Paul had wandered into the room of Chalky (Andrew Chalk) and Toks (Ian Tokins), two of the Madness road crew. Chalky and Toks had a double act that the Chuckle Brothers might have been proud of, or the two grumpy, piss-taking old boys from *The Muppet Show*.*

---

* Chalky and Toks stayed with the band for several years before getting sacked by the management. They'd had two warnings and knew that once they'd got the third they'd be told to leave, which us band members didn't like at all. Instead of waiting for their final warning, they resigned. I was sad when they did. They were lovely blokes and certainly helped to keep my feet on the ground. I should have rejected their resignation, in hindsight.

Chalky and Toks were the constantly cheeky masters of winding people up, including the Madness management. From what I heard, they saw Weller going into their bathroom, where he took a shower. While he was in the shower they nicked his clothes, hid them and, when he got out, kicked him out of their room. I suspect Paul just decided to style it out and thought, 'Oh fuck it!', legging it towards the swimming pool and jumping in. He probably did the right thing to save some face.

I saw Paul with The Jam again when Madness were in Japan. We just happened to be in the same hip bar, acknowledging each other but not really striking up a conversation. I've never been one to approach other celebrities as I'm fully aware their behaviour has the potential to shatter your perception of them.

Not that I'm saying Paul would have said or done anything to piss me off – besides which, I've heard that

---

Chalky: Toks and me kept Lee and the other band members' feet firmly on the floor. We could do that because we were all mates and we'd known each other for a good while. We all knew where we all came from. There were a couple of times on the 2Tone Tour when the Madness current management said something to Lee about us – but he saw through it, as the management were trying to find a way to cut off the band's roots. When I saw Lee starting to behave like a bit of a pop star, I was able to tell him to shut up. I'd remind him that he was Lee Thompson from north London and having some American record company licking your arse meant nothing. Lee respected that; he didn't mind being told when he was being a twat. There were many times when Toks and me could have been hoofed out, but credit to Lee and the band – they stuck with us because they knew we'd come up with them and we reminded them where they were from. All these years later I'm still friends with them. I think there are a lot of fans who have stuck with them because they still see Madness as their own, still getting away with it.

(Pennie Smith)

Freight train hopping to France, Oct: 74'

From left to right: Fredrick Thompson, day release, c53; Mum and me, 57; with Grandad; baby burglars, me and my cousin, c59; Tammo Land revolt, 66 *(PA Images/Alamy)*; Chafford School for Wayward Boys, 71; me, Mike and Si in France, 74; with Si on top of a factory, c74; my first girlfriend, Julie McQuade, c74; Barzo in the launderette freshly trimmed, c74; with Si outside the Hope & Anchor, 74.

From left to right: with my graffiti cans, Luton, c74; with Chris F, 75; with Deb, 75; with Si, Kentish Town Station, c75; with Paul C, 75; with Tony on the lido steps, c75; me, c75; boys are back in town, c75.

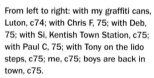

From left to right: Dolphis and Eddie Joseph, c74; with Uncle David, Aunt Cherry and cousin Vince, c76; Deb and Tracy, c75; hanging about in Luton, 76; first baggy trousers pose, Luton, 76; our friend Marion, Deb, me, c77; with Deb at Town & Country Club, Kentish Town, c75; with Dad watching the Bill Grundy interview, 76.

From left to right: Cathal and me posing, c75. Terry McQuade, Toks and Dixie; Harry Wandsworth, on tour; in Malta, 77; Toks, Chalky and our mate Lydsey (below), c79.

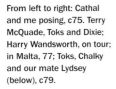

Dr Feelgood at the
Hope & Anchor,
August 76. Gigs
like this were a
massive inspiration.
(Chalkie Davies/
Getty); nutty boy at
the Madness press
conference, August 79
(Jill Furmanovsky).
Opposite page: Early
tour shot, 79 *(Gus*
Stewart/Getty);
with Bedders and
Chash, in the US of A,
November 79
(Ebet Roberts/Getty).

A fairly standard end to a
2Tone Tour show, November
79. Chris is the one in a
headlock courtesy of The
Selecter's Hammond organ
player, Desmond Brown
(Virginia Turbett/Redferns).
2Tone on tour, Brighton
Beach, November 79
(Chalkie Davies/Getty).

'Embarrassment' is his favourite Madness song, which is some compliment. (When he was with the Style Council, Madness sometimes played on the same bill – at CND and Red Wedge events in the mid-80s.)

I do remember being in the Mudd Club in New York City one night, when Pete Townshend was in there too. As much as I wanted to make a big deal of it, I tried to play it down and not approach him. But I was with Chrissy Boy at the time and he wasn't going to pass up the opportunity, so he asked Townshend if he wanted a drink.

"What will it be?", Chrissy asked, trying to be as calm and casual as he could. Townshend replied, "I'll take a VAT – vodka and tonic – off you please. One ice cube, none of that mad crushed shit." (I'll always remember that.)

On another occasion in America, Frank Zappa attended a Madness concert at the Mudd Club. Of all people, he'd come along to see for himself what these nutty boys were all about. But again, I refrained from going to meet him (he'd left earlier anyway!). Maybe it had something to do with when I first approached Ian Dury?

Going back to the 1970s...

Like I've said, I was quite blinkered in some ways back them. Although I recognised punk, and that change meant progress, I just didn't get too involved with it. It was to pass me by. But in hindsight, a lot of good music and fashion happened because of punk. Nothing much has really happened to youth culture since then; the acid-house thing of the late 1980s was possibly the last mass youth-culture movement. Things like 2Tone and grunge made some impact, but it wasn't huge. Nowadays, everything just seems to get thrown together into a massive melting pot. I think the music business is suffering and going backwards as a result.

For a group or artist to make any impact now, they need to have some kind of spectacular backing to get noticed. TV is awash with shows like *The X Factor* and *Britain's Got Talent*; it's what people are being fed and told that they need, but I feel like they're mocking the afflicted sometimes. I've been shown some absolutely terrible stuff on there and I've also seen some brilliant stuff – but it's not fair because most of the good stuff also loses out, as the panel are only voting for viewing figures. It's freak-show time.*

Going back to the 1980s...

There were lots of benefit concerts happening. I attended one at the Brixton Academy with some of Madness, where we got up on stage and jigged about with UB40.** Mike

---

* I've recently written a song about this very thing called 'BFS', which stands for 'British Film Standards' (but I'm also toying with calling it 'Pussy Galore'). It's a song about what goes on after the 9pm watershed. There have been times lately when I've felt like that Kenny Everett character, Cupid Stunt, telling myself it's 'all in the best possible taste!', even though it doesn't seem like it. I just think there's an absence of standards on a lot of telly at times. I felt like an old fuddy-duddy writing that song, but it was enjoyable and it got a few things off my chest.

** After the Brixton Academy received its 6am licence at the end of the 80s, it became a magnet for the 'E' scene and all-night raves. Reports say the ecstasy trade at the Academy was worth £1 million a weekend. The venue was situated too far south of the river for me. My equivalent was the Forum in Kentish Town, where Wendy May's Locomotion kept me on my dancing toes, as well as the House Of Fun nights on Saturdays. I was also the wrong side of thirty for ecstasy, which was too emotional a drug. I held out for shrooms a few years later.

Barson had now left the band, so it would have been during one of our 1985 'aimless periods'.

What I remember most about that night is ending up back at the hotel where UB40 were staying. For some reason I'd driven that night and had parked up in the road, directly outside the hotel. I had a Honda Prelude at the time, but when I went back to it the following day I discovered it'd been moved. It appeared to have been lifted up and carried to the other side of the road. (There was some building work going on so I assumed a few builders had bounced it over.)

Chris, Chas and Suggs had left a little earlier, which meant I was left chatting to an accountant and a lawyer. I was passed a joint, and after a few draws I felt very strange. Whatever it was, it wasn't grass. Though I *do* think I know what it was...

I was sat in front of these two fellas having a conversation about finances, investments and band lawsuits, and it was like a living nightmare. I could feel myself going back several years to the Big Ben episode. They were boring me to the point of chucking up. You know that feeling when your mouth waters up, so you swallow and your guts are contorting northwards?

I wanted to throw up there and then. It was just horrible; I had to really concentrate on not barfing over these gentlemen. I also started to sweat and knew I needed to get to a toilet.

I pushed myself up from the sofa, trying not to look like I was too much off my chummy. I spotted a toilet sign, 'Ladies', but this was an emergency. As I climbed the stairs I felt like I was sliding backwards. I eventually reached the toilet and, as I put my hand on the door handle, it seemed to melt.

Just as I managed to turn the door handle and push it open, Brian Travers, the UB40 saxophone player, called out to me. He was standing next to Chrissie Hynde, I think! Well, same hair and dress sense. Brian wanted to pull me into their conversation. As he yelled, "Oi, Lee!", all I could muster was a wave and mumbled, "Not now," as I fell backwards into the toilet.

I don't recall much more after locking the toilet door behind me. I don't know if I was sick or not, but I do remember losing control over some of my bodily functions and making a dreadful mess. I sat on that toilet for such a long time that my buttocks sank into the seat. It was very uncomfortable.

At some point the door was forced open and I was found with my legs up in the air, in a very sorry state indeed. I think it was Brian who managed to pull me off the toilet and re-dress me, making me look half-decent again. I must have had another black-out because I don't remember returning to the party, or talking to anyone else. All I remember is waking up in Brian's bedroom, fully dressed. Thankfully, I hadn't shit myself and the sheets were clean.

Brian was sleeping in the room too. I sat up, wiped my eyes and noticed some boot polish on top of a bag. Well, feeling a bit more like myself, not wanting to miss an opportunity, I grabbed the tin, quietly prised it open and dipped my finger into it. I then crept over to where Brian was sleeping and, pretending to wake him up, wiped this black boot polish onto his face. *Bullseye! Hit it!*

Brian must be a heavy sleeper because he didn't stir at all. I couldn't wake him so I decided to just leave. The last thing I did as I exited the bedroom was take a final glance. My artwork on his nose, cheeks and chin looked pretty good, so I left feeling quite pleased with myself. Amazingly, I had no raging hangover either...

7

No Money

I took my driving test in July 1976. It went okay, but by the time I took it I had a fair amount of driving experience already. I'd had several motors prior to settling with a Morris 1000 van: Humber Sceptres, Sunbeam Rapier, 1963 Hillman Minx, Zodiac with bench seat. At the time you'd pick them up for fifty or sixty quid. The insurance cost more than the motor.

Morris 1000s weren't the best designed cars and the footwell area would rot away, but they were great if you were carrying tools or musical equipment. There were times when I could actually see the road through the gaps though. Mike had one too, with exactly the same problems. Somehow that van used to get through its MOT, so I always had wheels to get around on.

I used that Morris 1000 for work. I provided a window-cleaning service and did the odd bit of gardening too. I had that van around the time when there were lots of strikes. The dustmen were among those striking for better conditions, more money, all the usual stuff. But people still needed their rubbish gone, so I'd collect it for them and get rid of it.

I never did any fly-tipping with those bags of rubbish. I distinctly remember going to the tip at Summers Lane in Finchley. It was me and Carthal 'Chas' Smyth who supplied this unique private service. We considered ourselves to be quite the entrepreneurs back then and would come up with all sorts of ideas to make a few quid. Some came off and others didn't.

Chas was always coming up with ideas – but then he's an ideas man. We first met in a pub called the Duke of Hamilton that we both used to frequent in Hampstead. He was friends with John Hasler, who became a big part of Madness in the early days. There was a crowd of us that would meet up in that pub. It was very sociable and, at that time, nothing to do with music. It was all teenage kicks and after-pub parties. I had started going out with Deb at this point, and she was not really into the Hampstead set, or the Hampstead girls! She seemed to get on with one or two, such as Jane Hill from Belsize Park.

Suggs also used that pub, and he and Carl had a very similar sense of style. In time, we all started dressing the same way and discovered that we also had the same musical interests, too.

Carl and John both lived in Muswell Hill. I think they'd see one another around the streets. John's dad was a well-known pillar of the community, very upright and respected – a policeman. Carl's dad had a job that took him all around the world. He was in the oil industry and this required the family to live in lots of weird and wonderful places, before they eventually settled in Muswell Hill.

I felt that Carl and I had a lot in common, especially when it came to music and fashion. We got on well and had a laugh together. If I discovered something new and presented it to him, he'd like it; if he found something new and showed it or played it to me, I'd like it too. I have a lot of many joyful memories of being in Carl's company – both before Madness and when the band got going.

But we were often like two sticks of dynamite waiting to go off. Working together was always eventful. There were times when we were window cleaning when he'd be gripping the back of my jeans as I hung from some second-floor apartment.

I did some gardening jobs with Carl, but the majority of that work was done with Chris and Mike. We worked for a proper company called Your Gardens Ltd, based in Mill Hill. I first started working for them over the Easter period in 1974, then decided not to go back to school.

It wasn't until September that Chris started to work for Your Gardens full time. Soon after, I left to work for Camden Council's parks and gardens, in the hope of becoming a tree surgeon (which obviously never happened!). Mike Barson did a stint with Chris for Your Gardens too. He had his van, so they'd go off and do gardening jobs – mostly just maintenance and clearance work, nothing too spectacular. It wasn't like we were designing landscape gardens.

I did a little bit of landscaping work though, and found it quite interesting. My teacher was Ray, a very patient fella who, for a hobby, used to dig up Victorian R. White's

Lemonade bottles from old landfills. The bottles were sealed with glass marbles and he'd sell them from a stall at Dingwalls market.

I also remember doing some stonework. One day I was cutting some York Stone and a splinter came off and hit me in the eye. I had to go to Moorfields Eye Hospital to be treated. Madness were going by this time and we had a gig that night at the Dublin Castle. Before I left Moorfields, they handed me some glasses and told me I had to wear them for three days. They were big and dark – similar to what Ray Charles would have worn.

I had to do the gig that night wearing those glasses. Because of the darkness at the Dublin, I could hardly see anything. But Moorfields had put some drops in my eye to dilate the pupil, so the strength of the light was magnified tenfold. I couldn't take those glasses off because of the intense brightness!

Doing that gardening job was straightforward. It freed me up to do the Madness rehearsals and gigs. At the end of the week I collected my little brown envelope with £11 in it, which meant I could have a fantastic weekend and blow pretty much all of it.

Getting a wage packet was a lovely feeling. Things seemed simple back then. You'd pay your rent, buy your fags, go to the pub, see your mates, get a bag of chips and have a great time – before starting it all again on Monday morning. It was a very working-class way of life.

Going into business or working for myself did not attract me one bit. I was young, free, had my girlfriend, my job and a good bunch of mates. Fantastic!

I was eighteen back in 1975, and in four years times I'd be my own boss – on the board of directors, employing a truckload of people in the music business. And I wouldn't wish that upon my worst enemy! How ironic...

But I liked the feeling of opening the van doors up, pushing all the gardening tools to one side, loading up with amps and musical instruments – or sometimes the band members – and heading off to play a gig somewhere.

In early '78, I was offered my first council flat on the Caledonian Road. This was shortly after squatting in the top-floor flat I'd decorated for the council on the Hampstead Road Estate – a six-storey block with a lift that didn't work, a real pain to get up and down with your tools and ladder. When the council moved me on, they told me the flats were being offered to elderly people downscaling. I thought that was typical of the council, given that the lift was rarely in operation.

Before that, I'd live in a few squats and stay with a few people. I was a bit like the bed-and-breakfast man for a while, before getting that council flat with Debbie. It was easy to stay with family and friends, or find squats in the NW5 area. It's virtually impossible in cities like London today – all the regeneration has left homeless people sheltering in shop doorways, back alleyways and park areas.*

---

* I've recently had a young lad staying at our home. He's a mate of my son Kye and has had troubles with his stepmother, resulting in him getting kicked out. He's a lovely kid, he has a job, but he has absolutely nowhere to stay and can't afford a place of his own. He's been sofa surfing and currently spends a couple of days with us. He drags all his belongings around in a few dustbin liners and, at the moment, hasn't got much of an opportunity to improve his situation.

The place that Debbie and I were given was a one-bedroom basement flat in an old Victorian house. It was tiny but in a good condition. I thought I'd cracked it as I now had the band, a job, and Debbie and I had a place that we could call ours.

The flat was walking distance to the opticians where Debbie was working, so it suited her. Between us we had enough money coming in to pay the rent and live comfortably. It was quite a romantic time, as if Debbie had brought back rose-tinted glasses from the opticians.

We were nicely settled in our flat and things were going well, until we got robbed. Madness were signed to Stiff Records by now, and we were out on the road. The robber took some of my personal belongings, like my prized records. They also stole my baritone saxophone that I recorded the *One Step Beyond...* album with (in tune too). I don't know how they concealed that as they legged it off down the Caledonian Road.

Because I was away with the band and Debbie was with me, it was my mother-in-law who was looking after the flat for us. She'd pop in a couple of times a week just to keep an eye. It was the first time that Madness had gone on tour in Europe and one of the local newspapers in London had written something about it. I was in Amsterdam when I got the phone call telling me the flat had been broken into.

It wasn't until I got home that I was able to find out what had been nicked. I was devastated.

Word got around about the flat being robbed and someone provided me with a description of who might have been involved. I know who that person was and if he's reading this, I still want my record collection and saxophone back. In fact, I'll even pay you...

Not long after the burglary, Debbie and I moved to a new flat in Denyer House. It was an unofficial swap with my uncle that was made bureaucratically official by the council about two years after we moved in! I was pleased to be back on my manor and Uncle Jack was pleased because he was a street trader in Chapel Market, only a short walk away from the Caledonian Road, his ex-missus and his daughters.

8

House Of Fun

There's a scene in *Take It Or Leave It* which shows me in Topsfield Road, near to where Mike Barson lived. I'm seen whistling for Mike in an attempt to get his attention. That was exactly the kind of thing I had to do, because Chris's dad and Mike's mum didn't like me going around to their homes.

I think Mike's mum considered me a bad influence on her son, saying only that it was fine for me coming over for band practice as she knew we'd be off the streets. But what she didn't know was that Mike could get up to enough mischief by himself. He certainly didn't need me to lead him astray...

The house in Topsfield Road was where Mike lived with his two brothers and his mum. It must have been tough for her bringing up three lads on her own, so I can only imagine that she felt very protective and did what she thought was best.

Mike's older brothers were also musical, so his home was a very creative one. There was always a piano in the home and I believe Mike had lessons when he was a boy. (I don't know if Mike's mum was a music teacher, but she was a teacher in a school. 'Twas never discussed!)

The Barsons were a very bohemian family and, when I was allowed around their house, I found it to be very laidback and very arty. It wasn't like anything back at home. They even used brown sugar!

It was only when I got a saxophone and Chris got a guitar that Mike's mum started to accept me a bit more. I think she quite liked the idea that we were starting to do something creative and, if we were rehearsing in Mike's bedroom, she at least knew where we were.

That scene in the film shows Chris and me with Mike in his bedroom. There are records playing and a Fats Domino album on display that we refer to as part of our rehearsal. This is pretty accurate, as we did put on records from the likes of Fats Domino, The Coasters and Chuck Berry to play along to – or at least try to.

During this period, rock'n'roll was what we liked and what we listened to. I remember playing along to 'Poison Ivy' by The Coasters and 'Lover Please', Clyde McPhatter's version that Mike played me on his cassette recorder. It was fun stuff to play, and when Madness did one of our Butlins weekenders* we relearned and performed a bunch of those songs.

I believe we still had a set list from 1976 that had some of those rock'n'roll songs and we used it as our reminder.

---

* We were contracted to play a weekend in mid-November for a period from 2010–20.

In the sleeve notes on *Complete Madness*, there's an old set list that shows what sort of songs we played in those very early days. There wasn't any reggae at the time; that came later on. I think the first reggae that found its way in was The Cats' version of 'Swan Lake' from the late 60s. I liked that record – along with 'The Liquidator', 'Young, Gifted And Black', 'Montego Bay', 'Band Of Gold' and, hurtling in from another corner, Lee Marvin's gravelly, dulcet-toned delivery of 'Wand'rin' Star' – from my skinhead days at Alexandra Palace skating rink.

The process of learning songs in Mike's bedroom was quite awkward and time-consuming. We didn't have access to music books. Nowadays, you can go online and buy a book, or watch footage on YouTube and learn pretty much any song by any artist. The best Mike, Chris and me could do was play the record, listen to it, try to work out the notes and chords, and scribble down the lyrics.

(Having said that, I still own an Elvis Presley book and a Chuck Berry book from back in the day. The Elvis book is actually songs by Leiber and Stoller, who wrote a lot of the rock'n'roll and R&B that we played.)

Some songs were easier to learn than others. I remember us putting on Fats Domino's 'Shu Rah' and having to play it back over and over again. It didn't always come easy and at times it was a nightmare. It was probably the hardest work for Mike who had a better command of his instrument than Chris or I, so he had to be patient. At times those rehearsals bred tension and frustration.

Another source of frustration was the saxophone. Neither Mike, Chris nor I knew anything about how a sax should be tuned and how this differed to the tuning on Mike's piano. For instance, it meant that if Mike played a C then it would be a D (one tone up) on my saxophone. And that's just for a tenor sax because it changes again for other types.

We just didn't know any of this stuff. During those early rehearsals, I played out of tune while I learned to play the sax. I didn't know any better. It wasn't until Clive Langer started to record Madness that I discovered how to tune a saxophone.

Along with the sense of frustration hanging in the air, there was also the stench of boys in Mike's bedroom – that young teenage smell that only boys can exude. That's what we breathed in as we learned to play those songs. Fortunately, we also had the smell of real coffee to defend us from those hormonal odours, which was wonderful. Like the brown sugar, it wasn't something I was familiar with.

At the time Mike's house was the perfect place for us to rehearse. We'd be left alone; there were invigorating odours, a piano, and nice pieces of artwork hanging on the walls. It was an environment that felt creatively untidy, at least compared to my home where Mum kept everything in a certain order. Despite Mike's place appearing to be in a bit of a mess, he knew exactly where everything was.

Those rehearsals would usually happen midweek. It was a matter of Chris and I jumping on a bus near Crouch End, instruments tucked under our arms, and heading to Muswell Hill, as neither of us had passed our driving tests yet.

We all had other things going on to occupy our time, so during that period there wasn't any real momentum behind us. We were far from regarding our instruments with any really serious intent. That would come, but not for a few more months. We were really just three mates messing around with a piano, a guitar and a sax.

Mike Barson: Lee, Chris and me were all really into music. Music was one of the most important things for us. We'd go and see a lot of bands and be amazed by the performances that they did. We found it really interesting. When a new album came out by one of the artists that we liked, it was a big deal. Getting the album was one of the ways we got our information about the artist or the band. It added to the excitement.

From being really into music, we then shifted from listening to it to starting to make it. I was already playing piano and I'd got music books that showed you how to play chords. I had an Elvis Presley one and a Tamla Motown one, and I learned the songs by using those books. Lee and Chris didn't play any instruments at first, but then they started to learn saxophone and guitar. There were times when it was a bit frustrating but it didn't really matter, because I always felt optimistic. I understood that learning an instrument is like trying to learn a new language – it takes time and it takes practice. You have to keep going and going, but in the beginning it was quite hard-going to try to play music with Lee and Chris.

What I didn't really know was that Lee and Chris were practising their instruments at home. Until recently, when we were doing our book *Before We Was We: Madness By Madness*, I never knew that when Lee went back to Luton he would take his sax into a field and practise on it. I just thought he was going back to Luton because he was losing interest in the band. It was short-sighted of me and I didn't really give him the credit.

Those bedroom sessions were happening around the time of pub rock, as punk rock was just starting to come in. This was the backdrop to what was happening in our individual lives, alongside our other interests – like getting into scrapes with our mates.

I was still getting involved with petty crime, but it wasn't anything too serious. Music was becoming increasingly important to me, it was just the distraction I needed. Music really took me in.

I had Mike and Chris to push me, as I'd push them. Then, when bands like the Sex Pistols caught our attention, it told us that if they could do it then so could we. That's when something shifted for us.

Those rehearsals round at Mike's were simple: a few mates got together to try to play some of our favourite music, have a cup of tea or crack open a can of beer. I have a lot of fond memories from those great days.

I also remember being quizzed by my dad about where I was going and what was I doing with my saxophone. Dads do that – I still do it now with my own two boys. And when I'd tell him I was heading off to rehearse with Mike and Chris, I think he actually quite liked it.

Maybe he just thought that at least I wasn't getting up to no good.

Those early rehearsals did serve as a more constructive outlet for my energies – and once I realised this, I wanted more of it. Despite the hard work it took to learn the sax, I stuck with it and got more serious about making music. But it also reached a point where Mike, Chris and me felt restricted. We knew we needed other people to join us.

Take It Or Leave It shows a meeting between Chrissy Boy and John Hasler in a job centre. I don't know if it actually happened or not, but there was some kind of encounter that resulted in Chris inviting John along to one of our rehearsals.

John Hasler: I met Lee before I met Mike or Chris. I would see Lee at the Bull & Gate, which was a pub in Kentish Town next door to the Forum. There was a disco in the pub called the Street Discotheque. It was a right dodgy place but it was popular at the time with underage drinkers. The landlord knew we were too young to be in there but he kept us out of sight and served us alcohol. I then met Mike through his brother's band, Bazooka Joe; I'd go and see them quite a lot. I then got to know the Aldenham Glamour Boys, who were linked to the youth club.

I would describe Lee at that time as being cheeky, quiet and friendly. He wasn't one of the hardmen from that group and a few of them had reputations. Lee had his own reputation though, and I remember a time when he stole his dad's car. It was a red one –

he wasn't old enough to drive at the time, so he didn't have a licence. It was actually quite comical because he struggled to see over the steering wheel, but we went for a drive around anyway.* This was the sort of stuff Lee got up to.

There's a scene in *Take It Or Leave It* that shows me bumping into Chris in a job centre and him inviting me to join the band. That never happened. I'd been living in Brighton as I wanted to get away from home. I got my first pay cheque and was thinking what to spend it on. I had my eye on a pair of leather trousers in a shop window – this was in the punk-rock days. There was another shop nearby that had a guitar in it. I was torn between the trousers or the guitar, but in the end went for the guitar. I was teaching myself basic guitar stuff and someone must have mentioned it to Lee, because on one of the occasions when I went back into London I saw him and he asked me did I want to be in his band? I agreed and went along to one of their rehearsals.

When I first joined the band it was just Lee, Chris and Mike. This meant there were two guitarists and none of us could really play much. We were really just making a noise. Around this time I'd sometimes go and hang out around Mike's house. His brothers were musical and they had a band that rehearsed in the house. Their

---

* I might have borrowed my dad's Vauxhall Viva, as he was 'working away'. But as for being too young for a licence, I was nineteen! I still didn't have one then though... I passed my test on July 12, 1976.

drummer left his kit there and one day Mike got on his piano and I sat behind the drums and just played. I laid down a basic beat and Mike said, "Look John, we've got two guitarists but no drummer..."

I replied that I didn't have a drum kit but I'd go and get one, and so I did. I got the kit off some bloke in Hampstead for sixty quid. It was black but I don't know who it was made by. It wasn't brilliant but it did the job. We'd have rehearsals in Mike's bedroom and because the drums were too loud, they'd drape shirts and towels over the skins to dampen the volume.

John lived just up from Mike at Muswell Hill. I don't recall how Chris knew him but we all frequented a pub in Hampstead. He was just one of those faces. We didn't know he could play the drums at all, but we got him down to a rehearsal and he played along with us. His timing was somewhat ropey but he did eventually get a drum kit. The drums were set up in Mike's bedroom and from here on rehearsals took on a whole new meaning for us.

When it had just been Mike's piano, Chris's guitar and my saxophone we could manage the noise levels okay, but having a drum kit suddenly thrown in caused problems for the neighbours. In an attempt to do something about it, we covered John's drums with bits of cloth – old t-shirts and tea towels mostly.

Despite damping down John's drums with towels, it didn't dampen his enthusiasm and he did his best. John helped focus us. He had something in his personality that pushed us and guided us.

Having a drummer also changed our sound – if we had any kind of a sound, that is. As a four-piece we sounded fuller, which was encouraging and gave us a boost. The band – although I don't know if we even thought of ourselves as that at the time – took on yet another dimension when we played with our first ever bassist.

Gavin Rodgers was Mike's girlfriend's brother. (I think he was an art student at the time; he later went on to become a journalist.) I don't think Gavin rehearsed with us at Mike's. We did use a church which was opposite Mike's art college; the vicar let us use the space for about £3.

That church suited us: it was easy to get to, cheap, and the vicar allowed John to leave his drums there. It also meant we could make a lot more noise than we ever could have back in Mike's bedroom. This opened up a whole new world for us as we experimented with our instruments.

As a five-piece we still played rock'n'roll covers. They were simple, three-chord tunes that we could have fun with. We weren't as yet driven by ambition, or consumed by the desire to become pop stars – or at least I wasn't. I quite enjoyed the challenge though. I'd suddenly gone from climbing up a tall lamppost or drainpipe to finding the correct notes to play on a Coasters song.

It still wasn't all plain sailing though. There would be times when Mike and I came to loggerheads whilst trying to work out a song. He'd get frustrated; I'd get frustrated; I'm sure Chris did too. The arguments between Mike and I have been written about in the other Madness books, and there's a scene in *Take It Or Leave It* that's meant to dramatise what happened.

It's true that there were times when heated arguments occurred. The exchanges between Mike and me became more frequent as we got more serious about what we were doing. Mike also dropped out of art college, partly because he started to take music more seriously. With this new direction and focus came new ways of thinking and new attitudes. It was often these that fuelled the arguments.

At one stage, things actually got so serious between us that Mike got another sax player in. This hasn't been written about and it wasn't depicted in *Take It Or Leave It* either, but that other player auditioned round Mike's house. I remember he had that rockabilly look, an Andy Mackay type of appearance. He also had a very shiny saxophone and he could actually play it.

Of course, I was feeling threatened. However, he only lasted one rehearsal until normal business resumed. This was partly because I caught the guy putting some of Mike's singles under his coat and making off with them. I remember not quite being able to believe it, but it happened. Just after he made his exit I told Mike, who chased after him and retrieved his records.

That guy is still around and I've seen him play a few times. He's really good, but he didn't end up being the saxophone player in Madness.

Without a doubt it was Mike who first started to take the whole thing seriously. It took Chris and me a bit longer to catch on. It affected the relationship that the three of us had in different ways. We'd gone from being mates who'd get up to stuff like graffiti and going to see bands together. They'd been there for me when I was shipped off to Chafford Approved School, but now we were three mates in a band together. We hadn't seen that coming a year or two earlier. But it was a really fantastic time, with a guiding light appearing somewhere along the way.

It was Mike pushing us to rehearse. I can hear him now, repeating: "Are you coming to rehearsal? Are you coming to rehearsal?"

This was happening during the period when I was still living in Luton, at Debbie's, or with my uncle. It wasn't always easy to get to rehearsals, but I tried my best. There would be times when I'd get the train down from Luton, we'd have a rehearsal and then I'd stay at someone's home before getting the train back the next day. But as I got more serious about playing the sax and being in a band, I'd try harder to make things work. It drew me back to north London, which is where I knew I needed to be.

Debbie had got me my new sax, so I'd gone from a battered old Boosey & Hawkes to a really good Selmer Mk6. I felt ready to make changes, to commit to getting serious. It was then that I decided to make a real effort to become a saxophone player – with some help from my friends.

Out of all of us, it was Chris who found it the most difficult. Unlike Mike and me, he had responsibilities. He had a son, Matthew, and his wife wanted Chris to have a nine-to-five that was secure and stable, bringing in a regular income.

I felt that Mike and I were pulling him one way and his wife another. On one occasion, she hung his guitar out of the window of their council flat to wind him up as he now had two guitars, so he went in and smashed up that first guitar he'd got from Camden Town. Thankfully though, Chrissy Boy wasn't warned off and we all got stuck in even deeper.

It must have been tough for him at times but, like Mike and me, he was keen to take it more seriously. Plus we were three mates, so being in a band meant having fun.

I was fortunate to have Debbie. She never gave me any problems or put any pressure on me. If anything, she encouraged me by buying the Selmer. But we didn't have anything like a mortgage, or any kids that we were responsible for, so our situation was very different to Chris's. Debbie came along to some of the early rehearsals, sometimes with a friend called Kirstin who was a lovely woman. (Kirstin lived close to Mike and was his girlfriend; her brother, Gavin, was our bass player.)

Still, the arguments at rehearsals continued between Mike and me, despite moving out of his bedroom and into the church hall. It was never anything too serious but there were some things about him that grated. I suppose there were some things about my personality that wound him up too...

Debbie: We would go to Mike's house when they were rehearsing. They'd sometimes be in another room, which meant his girlfriend and me would stay in Mike's bedroom, amusing ourselves by going through his drawers. At the time they were just mates playing a few songs together. I wasn't looking too closely at what they were doing, but I could see they enjoyed it. They all got along so there were never any really serious conflicts.

I do remember that Lee used to storm out the most though. I think he'd get frustrated and it'd get the better of him. He wanted to be able to play his saxophone and he made the effort and took the time to learn it, often on his own where no one could hear him. Luton allowed him to spend hours practising.

At times Mike could be what I'd describe as 'direct'. He has that quality in a person that gets things done; sometimes, to achieve that, you have to be very focused and very determined. It's just that being like that can sometimes rub others up the wrong way. But Chris and me needed Mike to be that way; if he hadn't been like that, then maybe there would never have been a Madness.

Some of the disagreements that Mike and I had resulted in me leaving the band for a period. This did happen quite often, although not on a weekly basis. Sometimes it was just the practicalities of getting into London from Luton that interrupted things.

Debbie: On one occasion, Mike, Lee, Chris and me were driving in this old GPO [General Post Office] van that they had. We were on our way to Luton and this was the first time I remember Mike saying they needed to do a gig. Lee and Chris's response was a sort of "No, we're not ready for one," but Mike felt very strongly about it and it was obvious that he believed they were.

Despite not being 100 per cent up for a debut show, we continued with rehearsals. Gavin played just one gig with us before he left, which was at his house in celebration of his sister Kirstin's birthday. It was his first and only performance, in April 1978.

(It's been written that this gig happened at Si Birdsall's house, but it didn't. We had no bassist at Simon's house party.) We were still a long way off from being called 'Madness' at the time, but there's actual film footage that survives of us playing. This was Chris, Mike, Gavin, John, Suggs and me – soon after that Suggs was gone, but he'd be back.

Toks: I knew Lee years before I got involved with the band. I used to see him around areas like Tufnell Park. He was a few years older than me and one of the older Aldenham hooligans. This was a couple of years before we all started to dress like skinheads. It was around 1975 and we were more into wearing bowling shirts. Lee always looked pretty cool. He had a sense of style. We didn't really know one another – we were more on nodding terms when we passed each other in the street.

I had a mate called Dixie. We both got into being skinheads around 1977 and we'd go to punk clubs too, like the Vortex and the Roxy. Dixie, like a lot of my mates, had a habit of spray-painting his name on walls. We started to notice some graffiti that said, 'Suggs Super Skin' or, 'Suggs is our leader' and think, 'Who the fuck is he?' Then one night we were down the Hope & Anchor and someone introduced us to Suggs. We became mates after that. It was from our connection with Suggs that I got to know Lee properly.

The gig we did at Simon's place happened later. By this time Mike had split up with his girlfriend, Araxi, and was now seeing Gavin's sister Kirstin. Araxi had a brother called Dikran Utidjian (stage name Tulaine), who landed up doing this one 'back garden gig' as our singer. He was a bit of a James Dean character and went on to have a career in films. Suggs was also there to watch our performance with some skinhead friends, perched on a very precarious garden brick-wall.

We were meant to play inside the house, but for some reason we ended up having to set up all what little gear we had in the garden. This didn't go down too well with us and Mike pulled Si about it. But it was too late by then, so we played our set under the London night sky. We were calling ourselves The Invaders by now, which was a name Mike had come up with. He wrote 'The Invaders' on the bass-drum skin. It had a lightning bolt passing through it and looked fantastic.

John Hasler: This was really early on and my bass-drum skin had the lightning bolt going through the words 'The Invaders'. Gavin 'Plum' Rodgers would have been playing bass. The set would have included songs like 'See You Later, Alligator' and 'Shop Around'.

We played other gigs as The Invaders at the City and East London College and another in a youth club near Warren Street; there was also a gig in a pub called the Nightingale and one in a place that sold flowers in Hampstead High Street. It was during that gig that someone lobbed a beer can and it hit me on my head. There were a few teddy boys that turned up and they didn't like it when we started to play reggae. They'd been alright with the rock'n'roll songs. Lee only played at the Nightingale pub gig though.

Chalky: The band did a gig at some flower shop's lock-up. It was like a warehouse unit where things got stored. That night I went around collecting money in a plastic glass. I kept some back, telling myself it was my wages, even though I had nothing to do with the band. This was a few months before I started being their roadie.

We soon found out that there was another band also calling themselves The Invaders, and they were signed up. It wasn't even that original a name – there had been an R&B band from Bermuda in the late 60s who released records under that name (though I don't think we knew it back then).

Our response was to call ourselves the North London Invaders for a short period. I think that by adding 'North London' we were trying to sound like Kilburn and the High Roads, but it was too long really and didn't survive more than a couple of gigs.

We were all tasked with coming up with band names. I came up with the Big Dippers, obviously inspired by the fairground ride, and then the Soft Shoe Shufflers, which didn't get much positive response and there were a few others that didn't stick either. I think song titles like Shop Around and Poison Ivy were also suggested, but they got a stern 'no' – although Madness later got the thumbs-up and that was a song title too.

John Hasler also had a stint at being our singer. He started off on drums and then, after we'd kicked Suggs out for missing rehearsals, had a go on vocals. Our drummer around that period was Garry Dovey – he and I didn't click, period. Mark Bedford had introduced Garry to the band. He was a good drummer, but a heavy one.

I can't even remember why I didn't get along with Garry, but we ended up having a bit of a to-do and he left. Back then I did have some hot-headed ways. And on this one occasion, during a rehearsal, I decided to launch myself across this little dentist's room into his drum kit, gashing my knee on a cymbal and bashing my head on the low ceiling. The noise this caused and the injury to myself made things all the worse.

I'd had a few drinks earlier at the Moonlight Club in West Hampstead and I was totally out of order. It was very out of character, but there must have been some underlying issues. Being pissed up didn't help either...

Debbie: I was at their first gig. It was a party like any other and I don't remember thinking the band were either good or shit. There was a lot going on that night and the band was still forming, really. But then, when I saw them as what would become the Madness line-up, with Suggs, Woody and Bedders, I thought, 'Ah, that's more like it, they actually do have something!'

The only thing that let them down was Lee, because he was wearing a really tight pair of tennis shorts and he'd drawn pictures of faces on his knees with a marker pen. I just remember thinking, 'Why does he have to look like a fucking idiot when the rest of the band look pretty good?' In time I realised Lee did stuff like that because of his shyness. It's actually easier for him to go on stage as someone else – but I don't know if this was a conscious thing with Lee. He still does it today and that's forty years after going on stage.

Mike Barson: I saw footage of a Madness concert and you could see that Lee likes to show off. Lee likes to be a bit 'out there' and enjoys doing the things you're not supposed to do, like climbing up the speakers on the stage or hanging upside down from poles. When I watched that live show I found Lee to be so entertaining, he was funny, he'd smile, he'd amuse the audience and you could see people responding to him. Being in Madness gives Lee the permission to be himself, and there's not many jobs where that can happen.

Toks: In the early days there was something about Lee that was a bit shy-ish. He could be really quiet. He'd change once he got on stage. It was like this from the early gigs. Lee was great to watch: you could see he owed a lot to his heroes, Ian Dury and Andy Mackay. I think Lee got nervous, so his stage performance was a way he found to deal with it. He'd put his shades on and become someone else, someone daft and silly. It worked!

I went to watch the band rehearse when they used the dentist's. It was just good to see my mates making music, it didn't really matter if it was any good or not. They only played covers; I remember Motown songs. Mike could play and the others just made noises. They were still learning their instruments at that time. I remember seeing Mike and Chris trying to sing too – John Hasler has a recording from one of those rehearsals which I had a copy of too, but have since mislaid. That would be interesting to hear again.

We moved on from rehearsing at the church too as we'd found a new place in a dentist's surgery on the Finchley Road. It was there that I'd jump over the drummer's kit, attacking him miserably!

Carl (Chas) also got involved with the band. We had him on bass for a while; he was another of our Hampstead pub associates and knew John Hasler pretty well. Carl getting involved was just another example of the band thing expanding, getting more serious. Along with Suggs and Carl coming into the picture, we also had Andrew Chalk, better known to us as Chalk Charmer. He was another of our mates and would later become one of our roadies.

It was around that time of getting a flat with Debbie, in 1978, that things started to come together for the band. We were getting more semi-professional, writing our own tunes. A lot of people had been involved: Gavin Rodgers had enough of playing bass and decided to leave; Dikran Tulaine left to pursue a career in acting; John Hasler would soon stop drumming because it just wasn't happening.

The combination of the various band members and the chemistry between us just didn't work out at first. However, this period did open up the doors for Dan 'Woody' Woodgate and Mark 'Bedders' Bedford.

Mark Bedford: I was performing at a function in William Ellis School I'd arranged with Chris and Mike, with John Hasler on vocals and Garry Dovey on drums. There was someone heckling from the crowd; Chris sidled up to me and said, "That's our sax player, take no notice of him." Later on, after finally meeting him at our rehearsal room in a dentist's basement, he offered me a lift and took me on a death-defying drive home in his ex-GPO Morris 1000 van, through the back-doubles of Hampstead; I asked him to drop me at South End Green's bus terminus. I always thought of that drive as an initiation into the group, a kind of 'welcome to the band'.

9

Tomorrow's Dream

Bedders and Woody came into a situation which overwhelmed them to some extent. Mike, Chris and me had been mates for a number of years, and we had our quirky ways. Mark and Dan were children of the 60s, though only four or five years younger than us, but it seemed like a big gap back then. We were from the 50s, all grey background and peasoupers.

This age difference did show in some ways. Bedders and Woody also came from different areas to us and had different life experiences. Woody's father was a photographer and his mother worked at the BBC. Out of us all, he was the mellow, peaceful one. There was a laidback feel about him – quiet, gently well-spoken and calming. His musical tastes were also different to ours. I think the only band we had in common was Roxy Music.

Woody's sense of fashion also differed to ours. He leant more toward the hippy style, or at least he wasn't too far from it. The first time I met him, he was wearing what looked like a tea cosy on his head, a trench coat and a loud scarf with bobbles on – with iffy patterns from far-off lands.

This scarf later brought a bit of controversy from the music press. Its back-to-front patterns looked like swastikas but were actually religious symbols from Tibet, or thereabouts. But my initial reaction to this spotty kid wearing a tea cosy on his head and a tent on his shoulders was, 'What the hell have we got here?'

Woody had been introduced to Mike, Chris and me by Bedders. To this day I don't know what their connection had been and how they'd got to know each other. When Bedders joined the band I think he was living up from the Rainbow Theatre in Islington; I know he'd gone to a school in Highgate Road, NW5, and Woody went to Haverstock in NW3.

I remember having conversations with Bedders and Woody when they told me about this graffiti they'd seen around: 'KIX'. They couldn't understand how I'd been able to reach some of those places, but I'd explain there were often times when I'd be hanging off a bridge with Mike, Chrissy Boy or Si holding onto my ankles.

All I knew about Woody was that he could play in a way that suited our style. My initial sense on meeting him was that I wasn't convinced, but when he got on the drums he fitted right in. From the moment he laid down those first beats I just knew he was right for us. He had what we'd been looking for, even though we didn't really have a clear picture in the first place.

Our new skinsman gave something to the sound we'd been developing. His style worked for us. He didn't play anything that was too busy or over the top, and to this day he still plays like that – solid, or KISS (Keep It Simple, Stupid).

Woody wouldn't be in the band for too long before he discarded the tea cosy and trench coat. (He hung on to his karma scarf though.) He started to dress like us, a baby-faced skinhead in Sta-Prest and bomber jacket.

Woody is quite unassuming, he's happy to just sit there in the background. As a player he's solid and sticks to the formula, with the odd snare or *boom-blap!* tom suggestion from Mike. When he has his moment to shine, he'll do what he needs to do and then fall back. He knows how and when to draw the line and won't outstay his welcome.

This possibly applies to all of the band. None of us push it too much and if we have a solo part, we do what we need to do and leave it there. When Clive Langer became our producer, he really helped educate us in this area. He'd often say, "Why play twenty notes when five is enough?" Clive helped to bring a strictness and simplicity to Madness, which contributed to our overall sound.

Bedders also has an easy-going way about him. If anything, he's a lot more introverted than Woody, quite the opposite to me. But then he's the sort of man who knows exactly what is going on at any time. He has a keen mind that sees things as they unfold, which applies to everything – whether it's playing bass or the business end of being in a band.

There were never any issues with Bedders when it came to Mike, Chris or me as the main writers in the band, pushing our ideas forward. He'd listen to us and support us, it felt like he was always on the same page. Bedders and Woody are the band's heartbeat of a tune.

Bedders was also very artistic and skilled as a graphic designer. To this day, he runs his own graphic design company in between recording sessions and tours.* I think he worked in this field at the time of joining Madness and it was only because we got successful that he shelved it to give the band his full attention. But I doubt Bedders ever regretted putting his graphic design career on hold back in the late 1970s, because he totally loves his music. It was as important to him as it was to all of us.**

What was to become Madness was now taking shape, now that Woody and Bedders had become official members. It wasn't exactly a smooth run though, with so many bass players and drummers involved. We even had Chas step up at one stage to play the bass, but that didn't work out. I don't remember exactly why but, like Suggs and me, he kept going AWOL.

That scene in *Take It Or Leave*, where Mike offers him a lift home but only partway, has some truth to it. I don't know what Mike's reasons were, but I think it pissed Chas off and he probably thought, 'Fuck 'em.' (Chas did come back later, but in a different role of course.)

---

* Recently, as the band were working on the artwork for the front cover of the Madness book *Before We Was We*, most of us took a step back and allowed Bedders to deal with it. We knew we could trust him to steer us towards the best possible cover design.
** Even now, when Madness are not working together Bedders plays with long-time buddy Terry Edwards who was with The Higsons – a band who were on 2Tone at one point. Bedders always seems to have something musical on the go whilst juggling time with his family and Madness. He's reliable, staunch and always up for getting involved.

Things in the band settled a bit when it was me, Mike, Chris, Woody and Bedders. John Hasler had taken on another new role, too, and then Suggs came along. There was a period when he, like me, was in the band one minute, out the next and then back again.

I don't remember Suggs' first rehearsal with us, so I don't know if he actually did turn up with a bottle of vodka in his hands, half-cut, as is shown in *Take It Or Leave It* – but he may have done. I don't think it happened in a rehearsal room, like the dentist's either, I think he first showed up at Mike's house because we'd still rehearse there on occasions.

Chalky: Suggs and me started to hang around Camden. This was mainly because of the market and it was the only place where we could get Levi 501s. Camden also had some good record shops. I think it was from Camden that Suggs got to know someone, who then knew someone else, and this connection eventually led to us getting to know Lee.

I remember when Suggsy was going to audition with some band, which turned out to be Lee, Mike and Chris. They were calling themselves The Invaders. It surprised me because Suggs couldn't even sing. He was just going to bluff it, which meant he'd fit in because all of the band were bluffers. I mean Lee couldn't play the sax, Chris couldn't play the guitar and Suggs couldn't sing. It was only Mike who could play.

On the day of the audition Suggsy and me went down to the King's Road and got pissed. We went to the audition and Suggs was offered the part. It was

184

after this that we all really started to knock about with each other. It just seemed like something to do.

Take It Or Leave It shows Suggs taking the vocals to 'See You Later, Alligator' – a classic Bill Haley and his Comets track from the 1950s. A lot of bands were covering songs from that period at the time. The American look and teddy-boy styles were popular: beetle-crusher shoes were everywhere; punk bands like The Clash loved wearing them. Malcolm McLaren had a shop in the King's Road called Let It Rock which had stocked loads of American rock'n'roll-related stuff – before he transformed it into SEX and kick-started the Sex Pistols' career.*

When I first met Suggs he stood out as dressing in similar ways to me. He was knocking about with Chalky at the time, who he'd been mates with for years as their parents all knew each other. They were both Chelsea supporters and would spend most Saturdays watching their team down at Stamford Bridge or away.

Suggs and me liked the same sort of music, including soul and ska. From the off, we got along and enjoyed each other's company. I found him to be very knowledgeable and articulate, despite at times pretending not to be. But then he was very down to earth and still is to this day.** His accent

---

* Mike's brother Dan was playing exactly that type of music in his band on the pub-rock circuit, Bazooka Joe. We'd go and see them as they were always really good to watch. During the recording of *One Step Beyond...*, Madness did a version of 'Rockin' In A♭', one of Bazooka Joe's songs.

** After all these years we still get together outside the band. I was with Suggs and his wife Ann, around their place recently. There were a few of us, ending up with the women sitting at one end of the table and the fellas

was neither east nor west London, more a very unique pronunciation that would find its way into Madness songs.

When Suggs joined the band he brought a whole new dimension to what we were doing. For my part, I instantly pegged him as being (in the words of Ian Hunter) one of the boys. It didn't matter if he could sing or not. I mean it wasn't as if I was the world's greatest sax player. What mattered to me was having a singer who wanted to put a few stories to music and enjoy every moment of being in a band. And wanted to enjoy every moment of life itself. There were no expectations other than that. In the bigger picture though, I might end up spending a lot of time with this fella. If we got

---

at the other. We were all telling stories and trying to better one another: one of the group told us about the time his dad drove a horse and cart over Chelsea Bridge. The horse got startled and bolted, charging off over the bridge and straight up the stone steps of the church at the end, where there was a wedding going on. It must have been mayhem.

Suggs loved that story. It was a rare opportunity to just sit back and let someone else do all the work. As the singer in Madness he's had to do so much live radio and media, it must be nice to have a break.

It had been a lovely evening with good cooking by Ann, good drink and good company. I was getting ready to leave when I picked up a pair of eyeglasses. Suggs said, "Hands off, they're mine!" I held them up and replied, "No they're not, they're mine," telling him the make, the colour and how they had distinct blue arms. I even put them on to test the strength, which was as I expected. "They're fucking mine, you leave them alone!" he came back, but I protested. It got to a point where he backed down and said, "Go on then, you can have them." "Have them?" I said, "They're mine!" and stuffed them into my coat pocket. I put it down to him having had one too many drinks.

We said our goodbyes and went home. The following morning, I strolled over to my table and picked up the glasses – beside them was another pair that looked exactly the same make, colour and strength. Bollocks! Suggs had been right all along. I sent him a video saying, "What are the chances of that?" To which he replied, "Ha ha ha."

as far as getting a record deal and going on tour, then we'd need to be mates. This turned out to be the case, as there would be many hotels and late bars along the way.

Thinking back now over the past forty years, I do not recall a single time when Suggs and me rowed. Okay, we've annoyed each other along the way; these things happen. The closest we've come to being at loggerheads was at a dinner round his place. We were discussing an article in *The Times* about the rise of fascism. Out of nowhere, it was suggested, as I interpreted, that I'd voted for some dodgy 'political' party back in the late 70s. This totally threw me. A pregnant pause ensued, then an old friend, (what's it all about) Alfie, broke into a Tommy Cooper gag...

I'd known Suggs for forty years, travelled the world with him, spending countless hours in recording studios, and who knows how many late ones at the bar! He surely knew me as someone who would in no way support all that nonsense.

As the evening went on, we worked through it. We can be very passionate about what's important to us and racism is just one of those aspects that we both abhor. What's important is that we both know where we stand on certain issues and when to stand beside each other. Barson is the band member who is the most outspoken on political matters, but Suggs is a close second. When he and Mike get into a discussion it can verbally kick off.*

---

* Several years back, Madness were booked to play at some fashion show in Paris. For some reason, Terry Hall was there too. (I remember that he actually smiled.) We all went out for a meal afterwards and politics found its way into our conversation. It got really heated and close to some of the

As an unwritten rule, the members of Madness try to keep politics and music separate. For the most part, this has been maintained. But both as men and as a band we've been in plenty of situations when our beliefs have been challenged.

When Madness broke through, we were surrounded by a lot of tension and friction. The late 70s was full of it and it was often reflected in the music of the time. The Specials, The Selecter and The Bodysnatchers also came through around the same time as Madness. They were the 2Tone bands but they were different to us in that they introduced politics, or what they saw happening around them in society, into their music. Think about Specials songs like 'Ghost Town', 'Racist Friend' or '(Free) Nelson Mandela'. I'd be fully aware of what I was letting myself in for when I accepted their invitation to play saxophone on 'Hey, Little Rich Girl'.

There was a lot of opportunity for people to clash in the late 70s and it wasn't just fought out in the political arena. You also had the mods, skinheads, punks and teds fighting each other, and anyone else that wasn't like them. I'd witness first-hand how fashion and politics merged at a particular gig in Aylesbury, Buckinghamshire.

Madness were booked to play a gig, the show sold well and the audience were up for it. But large gangs of National Front members found their way into the venue and it all kicked off between them and the Anti-Nazi League. I saw a lot of kids getting punched and kicked, and it wasn't something that me or any member of Madness wanted at our gigs. I found out

band members getting physical. But that's what happens when people feel strongly about something, giving voice to their thoughts and feelings.

after that it had all been pre-planned and those NF idiots had deliberately targeted our gig as an opportunity to grab some attention. The Anti-Nazi League had found out about their rivals' plans and had decided to make their own stand. It was inevitable that there would be conflict.

Tracy: Lee was a skinhead and really into that look and ska music. He liked seeing proper skinheads at Madness gigs, but he didn't like the ones that were into the National Front. I was at a gig once when it really kicked off between those who were into it and the ones that weren't. Lee definitely wasn't, he hated that stuff happening at their gigs. Lee was far from being a racist and the rest of the band were the same.

Harry Wandsworth (Madness 'merch' seller): There was a period when there'd be all these pro-Nazi skinheads turning up at Madness gigs. It was when the National Front were very active. They'd hand out leaflets to people in the audience and there were a lot of kids in the crowds. One night, Carl went up to some of those skinheads and asked them what they were doing. He basically told them they were fucking idiots, grabbed their leaflets and ripped them up. One of those skinheads was only a kid and I could see he was just being led by his peers. The next time I saw him was he was wearing a parka and mod clothes, and he'd got rid of the National Front stuff.

Toks: There were people starting to show up at Madness gigs that the band didn't really want there.

They were the skinheads into the National Front thing. It got to a point where they'd go to lots of other bands' gigs. I used to go and see Sham 69 but that had to stop because I wasn't into the National Front and I wasn't West Ham. At first it was great seeing the skinheads turning up at Madness gigs, but then it wasn't so great because of the trouble some of them would cause.

I remember seeing Madness support The Pretenders down the Lyceum and feeling really proud, because these were my mates. The Lyceum was a really good venue. Another time, when Madness played there on New Year's Eve, Chalky and me were handed a box of balloons and told to blow them all up and put them in this huge net that hung from the roof. The idea was that they'd be dropped onto the audience.

We got bored blowing these balloons up and got the idea to fill some of them with water. I can't remember now what number Madness were playing at the time – 'House Of Fun' most likely – but it was spot-on as the balloons dropped down. Some floated down as they should but the water filled ones fell directly onto the heads of a mob of skinheads that had been playing up. *Wallop!*

Whenever I saw aggro at a Madness gig it upset me. At times it sickened me too. Gigs were about playing music, watching a band and having fun. They were not meant to be battlegrounds.

The whole 2Tone thing that Jerry Dammers and The Specials set up was a conscious attempt to challenge the sort of racial and political rubbish that was going on. The 2Tone idea was superb – black and white, different cultures coming together to make music that transcended hate and indifference. The music that bands like The Specials, Bodysnatchers, The Selecter and others on the label (including Madness) were making was just brilliant.

The interracial thing was important and I loved to see bands like UB40 and The Beat breaking through too. The whole idea of 2Tone was great; it was founded just at the right time and I feel personally proud to have been part of it. 'The Prince' was a perfect song for 2Tone. It was a white fellow's tribue to his black mentor, and the label helped launch us to a whole new level.

I do wonder whether, if Madness had been more politically vocal about our beliefs, we'd have survived and gone on to have a forty-year career in the music business. A lot of bands who were that way didn't make it past the early 80s.

Back in 1979, if Dammers had offered Madness the opportunity to make an album on 2Tone, I'd certainly have grabbed it with both hands. But the deal was just one single and that's how it ended up.

10

Hey You!

Carl 'Chas Smash' Smyth lives in Spain these days. I rarely see him now and only then if it's band related. But he and I always got on fantastically well. We spent as much time socialising outside of the band as we did playing inside it in the 1980s and 90s.

In the early days of first getting to know him, Carl came across as a bit of a loner. I think he lacked certain attachments that the rest of us had, as he'd spent large chunks of his youth moving about a lot due to his dad's work in the oil business.

Personality-wise, Carl has a really gentlemanly way about him. He's extremely generous by nature and has a great sense of humour. He had all of these traits from the moment I first got to know him, when we drank in pubs in and around Camden and Hampstead. We'd continue drinking in those same places once Madness was up and running; we'd have meetings there after rehearsals and plot our world domination.

Toks: Something I remember about Lee was that he'd always seem to disappear. We'd all be on a pub crawl in Hampstead and Lee would start off with us, but then you'd look for him and he was gone. He certainly wasn't at the bar! And then a couple of hours and three pubs later, he'd reappear and no one would know where he'd been. There were plenty of rumours suggesting he'd been up to no good somewhere.

Suggs was already in our little gang by the time John Hasler introduced Carl to the rest of us. He was like us in his sense of style and in his choice of music, so it was inevitable that we'd all click. This was late '74 going into '75, several months before any of us (apart from Mike) had even picked up an instrument.

I remember going to see bands with Carl, including Deaf School and Bazooka Joe. We'd go to places like Dingwalls and the Electric Ballroom, all the pubs that had bands playing (like the Nashville and the Hope & Anchor) and college gigs.

Carl and I brought out the entrepreneurial spirit in each other. We had a go at collecting rubbish and that worked okay for a while. We then did window cleaning but that didn't work out quite as well. Health and safety wasn't our main priority. I'd often be dangling off of gutters, trying to clean the upstairs windows, and I don't even recall if we had a ladder.

Those sorts of ventures happened in between other jobs that I had. A couple included attempts at lorry driving but that wasn't really for me. I did those jobs in between living in Luton and bedding down in various places around

London. It was at the time when I'd be in and out of the band according to what argument I'd had with Mike, or just the practicalities of getting to rehearsals.

During one of those periods I even joined another band, called Guilt Edge. They had a fantastic singer called David Banks – very Springsteen-ish looking too – and they needed a sax player, so I got involved. But they played American Midwest rock and it wasn't really my thing. Despite having a few rehearsals, it didn't work out and I left.

David had an older brother, however, who was a bit of an entrepreneur with several things on the go. He had a lorry and told me to pick up a load of cardboard and deliver it to a recycling yard. I picked it up and was headed east London way – typically, I was running late too.

There was another fella with me but he didn't know the area any more than me. We were going left, right, up the same road again. There were lots of railway arches around the area and if there were warning signs about height restrictions, we didn't notice any. I drove into one of the arches and sliced the top of the lorry off. Fuck me, did it make a noise!

I lost that job and you'd think I'd learn a lesson or two about driving lorries. But I managed to repeat the performance when I got a job driving for a building firm that supplied plumbing material. I had the task of loading the lorry up with long copper pipes to deliver. I was supposed to leave the yard in Kentish Town and deliver the pipes to east London (again), but this time I didn't even manage to get out of the yard. I underestimated the exit and again took the roof off the lorry. I lasted three hours in that particular job – probably my all-time record.

Alongside the rubbish collecting and window cleaning with Carl, we were just two mates having a laugh. There was never any talk about him joining the band at that point. He'd already had a brief spell playing with us, but he didn't really know anything about playing bass. Mike used to write the notes on the neck of the bass guitar for him. It didn't work out for Carl or for us, but what did work was when he jumped up on stage during our sets.

I think it was when we got our residency at the Hope & Anchor when Carl first started getting up on stage with us. We'd been using the old Victorian pub located in Upper Street, Islington, as our go-to place and got on well with the landlord, John Eichler, who was a larger-than-life fella.

The Hope & Anchor was one of the best places for a band to play – Elvis Costello, The Jam and The Specials all played there, where the heat would engulf you. There was also a live album released in 1977 called *Hope & Anchor Front Row Festival*, including performances from bands like The Stranglers and XTC.

John saw us play, liked what he heard and offered us the residency. He was aware than when we played we pulled a crowd, which was good for his till. We also knew lots of people that drank in the pub. One of the reasons we started using it was because our mate Si Birdsall lived opposite.

Carl was also one of our crowd. I distinctly remember him jumping up on the stage, grabbing the mike and doing his 'Hey you, don't watch that, watch this!' bit. What he did was really amazing. He had quite a presence about him and Debbie was especially struck by what she saw. She even suggested to him that rather than jump off of the stage, he should stay up there with us and dance like he did when he was in the audience. After which, he did just that.

I have a very vivid memory of Carl showing up at a gig we did north of the M25. I'd phoned him a couple of days before to invite him to come along and do his bit on stage. He told me he was pumping concrete down in Kent on the day of the gig, but said he'd try to get there in time.

Madness were on stage when suddenly I saw the audience shuffling to create a walkway area. It was like Moses parting the Red Sea – I saw Carl strolling through, wearing his mohair suit and porkpie hat, looking like a million dollars. He jumped up on stage just in time to do his 'Hey you!' bit before we launched into 'One Step Beyond...'. The timing was perfect; it really was something incredible. It's one of my favourite memories of him.

Carl became a permanent fixture in Madness, adding a certain vibrancy both on and offstage. I've been accused of voicing the opinion that I didn't want him in the band, prior to signing to Stiff Records, but this is quite simply not true. (I don't know where this came from – maybe some journo wrote it and people started to believe it. Or maybe Carl heard something along those lines and misunderstood it.)

But, for the record, it wasn't true. I was more than happy having a seventh member in the band and Carl brought something extra to Madness. We idolised each other. He was my Clark Gable and I was his... well, Hilda Ogden.

The Hope & Anchor was good for us. It helped take us to the next level. I always enjoyed playing there because we'd see our mates too. There was a group of us all into the same fashions and music. It was like having our own little exclusive club.

The pub had a good jukebox too, which took a hammering. I recall how '96 Tears' by ? (Question Mark) and the Mysterians got played a lot. The Stranglers would cover that track – maybe they'd heard it on the Hope's jukebox during their pub-rock days.

We'd get a drink at the bar and then make our way down the narrow stairway to the basement and music area, where there was a modest stage. The ceiling was low and it would get very hot down there.

One night I wore a silly suit with a bowtie that lit up and a straw trilby hat. I had loads of badges pinned to the suit saying stuff like, 'Help Me! I Have Fallen Off My Seat And Can't Get To My Drink' and 'Old People Need Sex Too'. I'd be dripping in sweat as I tossed things into the crowd like old seven-inch records I'd bought or porkpies wrapped in Christmas paper. (I'd witnessed Davey Payne from Kilburn and the High Roads do similar things and thought it was very entertaining.)

I did get told off by John a few times, including for something that was particularly stupid. I'd smashed up a ping-pong ball and put all the tiny bits into wraps of tin foil. I then lit them and just as they caught alight, blew them out. It created a smoke bomb but the smoke it gave off was very intense, filling half the basement. People in the audience were bent over, choking and panicking as they scrambled to get out. The fumes were horrible but it soon cleared. I got a right bollocking for that though...

On another night in the Hope I wore a tennis outfit, stuck plasters on my legs and wrote stuff like 'Kilroy Was Here' on them. For some bizarre reason I even carried a tennis racket on stage with me and used it to bat tennis balls around the basement. There were balls bouncing off the walls, as well as off the heads of the audience. I really enjoyed this sort of stuff. The bollockings from John, or any of the other band members, never really bothered me too much.

One night I was placed near the back, next to Woody and slightly higher up than Chris at the front. The band were several songs in and I was happily blowing into my sax, with my eyes closed, when I heard a voice yell out: "Don't fucking do that!"

I opened my eyes but couldn't work out where it'd come from. I could see Chris glaring at me, but that was all. I just closed my eyes and carried on. Then I heard the voice: "Don't fucking do it again!"

I opened my eyes and the next thing I knew, Chrissy Boy donked me over my head with his Fender. The band were still playing but I shouted at Chris, "What's the matter?" He shouted back, "Stop spitting at me!" He thought I was gobbing on his head. I protested, saying it wasn't me, and pointed to the condensation dripping from the ceiling.

The Hope & Anchor never had any air conditioning. It was so bad that the mixing desk had to be covered in a plastic sheet. The risk was that water would get into the electricals, which could be dangerous or blow up our gear.*

---

* I went to a Jennie Bellestar gig once and stupidly, for a laugh, let off a fire extinguisher, left on the stage. I pointed it at the ceiling but it dripped down and started to fall on her guitarist's pedals. He was desperately trying to save his equipment from blowing up.

But I have so many fond memories of the Hope & Anchor. I loved John and that residency really did help us in our career. He'd even let us borrow his front room as a changing room when we returned there, in later years.

Despite the Hope having regular live music, there were times when the pub got into financial difficulties and the electricity got turned off. I went there once and the pub was lit by candles. We wanted to help John out so we played a gig at Dingwalls and gave the money raised to him, but its days were numbered. (I've been back there a few times though – it's now very comfy.)

I saw lots of bands at the Hope & Anchor: the Kilburns; Dr Feelgood; Elvis Costello – though I didn't stay for the whole thing, as it was so hot. It was not only an important place for bands from London. I believe Suggs and Mike saw The Specials in the Hope and were both blown away by what they heard and saw. They reported back that they'd seen another band that played the same sort of music as us, and even dressed like us.

I didn't make that Specials gig but, around that time, I did stumble across another band who were similar to us. They were called Bad Manners. I'd never heard them, I'd just seen their name in the live music section of *Time Out*. So I headed to Hackney Marshes, not knowing what to expect.

Bad Manners looked good, sounded good and were fun to watch. They had a brass section too, which certainly caught my attention. Musically, I thought Bad Manners were very 'nutty' – just like Madness. I instantly liked them.

I next saw them at the Hope & Anchor and got to know them a bit better, before Madness got them onto the same bill as us at the Electric Ballroom. I especially got on well with their singer, Doug Trendle, better known as Buster Bloodvessel. I even stayed with Doug when he had a squat in Stoke Newington – I had a lost weekend there, where I didn't know if it was day or night.

Bad Manners would have their fair share of hits with tracks like 'My Girl Lollipop' and 'Lip Up Fatty', and were also included on the 2Tone Dance Craze tour – even though they were never signed to 2Tone Records.

Doug and I knocked around for a while and he was fun to be with. I found him to be a very shy man, but charming and caring. Out of everyone from that period, he's the only band member I tend to bump into – sometimes in the most unusual settings.

Suggs had a chance meeting with Dougie too, down in Whitstable, Kent, one day. Suggs is happily tucking into some oysters whilst gazing out across the sea. Then he notices this huge figure rise up from the waves. The next thing, this big, bald lump strolls across the pebbles towards him and sticks out a tongue the size of an old Dr Marten boot, downs a handful of oysters, has a brief chat with Suggs and then turns to head back to the sea.

Lynn Milsom: It was 1979 and I going out with Brian Tuitt from Bad Manners. One night they were playing in a pub in north London. Lee was there. I had actually met him the week before, but didn't know who he was or even that he was in a band. I also saw a girl standing there and went over to ask if she was on her own. She replied, "No, I'm not, but I might as fuckin' well be, he's over there talkin' to them girls!" We hit it off from the start.

Madness and Bad Manners played together a couple of times at the Electric Ballroom, so I got to know Lee and Debbie better. Lee and Debbie were just such fun to be around. We were young and it was a really exciting time seeing Madness taking off.

It was a good time to be part of a bigger scene with bands like Bad Manners and The Specials. I was fortunate to get along with all the other band members. On the 2Tone Tour, Terry Hall and his girlfriend, who was very goth, polite and unassuming, were a bundle of laughs backstage after shows. Well, they'd have a right laugh at me, because I'd be the one pranking around while they drank coffee and I necked whatever alcohol was available.*

---

* I'm still friends with everyone today, though I don't see people as much because we're all still working. The Specials are playing still and from what I hear, their shows are second to none. I did have a laugh recently though, when Suggs showed me an interview with Terry, Horace Panter and Lynval Golding in *Q* magazine. The interviewer asked them if there was any competition between The Specials and Madness, to which Terry responded by saying that they'd had a hit with 'Ghost Town' but Madness had a hit with a comedy record. I thought it was funny but Suggs wasn't too amused, especially when Terry (or maybe it was the interviewer) compared us to the Barron Knights.

When I got home that night, I went on eBay to find a Barron Knights record where they were all dressed as clowns on the cover. It arrived a few days later; when it did, I got Debbie and my sons to sign it in the names of Madness band members. Daley then took the record with him when he went to see The Specials at the Forum in Kentish Town, passing it on to their tour manager. I've not had a response yet but I'm sure they had a laugh about it.

The Specials used to do a version of our signature tune, Prince Buster's 'Madness'. You can find footage on YouTube of them performing it on one of the *Rock Goes To College* shows, but I saw them do it when we were all on the 2Tone Tour together. It was the last night of the tour and we were leaving. We actually walked across the back of the stage, our bags over our shoulders, while they were playing the song.

I can only imagine that The Specials have fond memories of the Hope & Anchor too. But they didn't play there as much as us and didn't make a video there either. We did – 'One Step Beyond...'.

This came about in part because John Eichler knew Dave Robinson of Stiff Records very well from the pub-rock days. The Hope & Anchor had been very important for those bands. Another reason why 'One Step Beyond...' was shot there was because there was next to no budget available. An independent label like Stiff just didn't have the money to make glamorous music videos. Dave would have got the Hope for free and John would have been more than happy to help out.

Dave got in an American director called Chuck Statler, who'd made music videos for Devo, Elvis Costello and the Attractions and Nick Lowe. We actually ended up making two videos in one day: the Hope & Anchor scenes for 'One Step Beyond...' and all of 'Bed And Breakfast Man', which was filmed in the Clarendon Hotel in Hammersmith. The old Victorian hotel had been a music venue since the 1950s and would continue until the late 80s before closing its doors. (In its time bands like U2, Ramones and Pulp performed there.)

The hotel had a two-tone patterned carpet in one of the rooms. We set the band's equipment up on it and were filmed as we performed the song. I was dressed in a white t-shirt, my black leather jacket, red trilby and dark glasses. The filming was straightforward enough, but the 'One Step Beyond...' video was more involved.

We'd actually played a gig in Leeds, where we were filmed doing the Nutty Train down the street. We are also filmed coming out of a gentlemen's hairdressers called Alec's, but the rest of the 'OSB' video was made back at the Hope & Anchor. I think Chuck did a pretty good job of filming two videos in two days considering the Leeds to London minibus run down the M1.

The 'One Step Beyond...' insert for Madness' first video compilation promo starts with the band humming the tune, sat on the stairs that led down into the Hope & Anchor's basement. In those days the walls were covered in chalk scribbles. As the band sway from left to right humming their respective parts, I pop up at the front and croak the out of tune sax riff, before the actual song kicks in, with Chas doing his 'Hey you, don't watch that!' bit.

Then there's a young rude boy appearing from under the bedcovers. He was a lad who'd come to our gigs and always position himself right in front of the band. He loved us, so I can only imagine being featured in the video was a big deal for him.

There are a few herberts in Madness videos. One of them (in the 'Bed And Breakfast Man') we nicknamed Joe 90 because of his specs, seen punching the air in his braces and tartan Brutus shirt. He was a nice enough kid – I suspect he went on to become a medical professor or something similarly upstanding.

Then there was a third lad we called Prince Nutty, seen cracking away outside the red phone kiosks in a cap, specs and Crombie. There was also a brief shot of our roadie Chalky Charmer dressed in white t-shirt, jeans and loafers, sharing some excellent footwork. That dancing got copied countless times by young kids in their youth clubs and school discos. It lives on today, as you'll often catch sight of grown men doing it at our concerts. (I think Prince Nutty went on to carve out a career as a security guard.)

The 'One Step Beyond...' video was responsible for introducing the Nutty Train to the masses. 'Nutty' was a term that I came up with and it has stuck with the band. It described us as a gang of mates and our sound perfectly. In my mind, the Madness sound was something along the lines of the theme to *Steptoe And Son* meets Kilburn and the High Roads. I can also hear echoes of early Split Enz and some of The Kinks, but I think there was something quite old fashioned about us.

It was familiar. People could find something in our sound that they could either jig to or relate to. I could hear a lot of these references but had difficulty relaying it to the rest of the band. Mike helped to draw it out.

I have songs from that early Madness period that have never been recorded. They're my attempts at creating that Nutty Sound I heard in my head. One of them is called 'Jump In The Back Of The Jag'. Suggs knows it and keeps pushing me to complete it, so that Madness can record it. It's a song about the kidnapping of some gangster fella by a couple of removals men by day/doormen by night. The lyrics are based on the things that are going through the characters' heads at the time. It's very comical, in a white-knuckle way:

> Jump in the back of the Jag, we're going for a spin.
> Meet me sidekick Eddie and his big brother Jim, they
>   ain't a bad pair of lads,
> Once you get to know them,
> If you got to know them.
> My, my, you're looking kind of pale,
> Do you want the window open? You're sweating from
>   head to tail.
> And I can swear I can smell one terrible smell, here Ed,
>   can you smell that smell?

It didn't get much further than that. Maybe we'll get around to finishing it one day. I'm sure Chris and Mike will be able to come up with something musical.

Those words, 'Nutty Sound' or 'Nutty Boys', started to get used all over the place. The music journalists loved it as they were able to hang so much stuff on them. I had the words 'That Nutty Sound' bleached on the back of my Levi denim jacket. I was gutted though, because it burned through it just like bleach can do...

Mike wrote 'That Nutty Sound' on the rear doors of his van and also around the rim of his hat. He wrote it in a silver pen, along with musical notes going round and round.

We also recorded tracks with the word 'nutty' in it. 'The Nutty Theme' was used on the B-side of 'One Step Beyond...' and we also did 'Animal Farm – The Nutty

Sound', which was a crazy-sounding instrumental. In 1981, Stiff issued a twelve-inch under the title *Madness As The Nutty Boys*: it included 'Baggy Trousers', 'The Return Of The Los Palmas 7', 'One Step Beyond...', 'My Girl' and 'Night Boat To Cairo'.

As a whole, the band didn't mind us being associated with anything nutty. Personally speaking, I was really happy about it. 'Nutty' is still as relevant to us now as it was back in 1979.

11

The Prince

Although Madness were starting to take off, we were mostly still in the rehearsal stages with the occasional gig. I still wasn't making enough money to live on. I had to do different jobs to bring in extra cash. I was back and forth with the gardening work and that was alright, but it didn't make me a fortune. I then met some Polish guys who were plasterboard joiners. I started working for them and was pocketing something like twenty quid a week, which was an okay wage back in the late 70s.

I remember it was winter when I started working with those guys, because it was fucking freezing and the plaster would ice up. Within a few months I left because I thought I could start up on my own, but I held on to some of the tools. I then brought Suggs in to help me. I had my Morris van, tools and a bucket, and in my mind I was practically a qualified plasterer.

I got a job and Suggs came along on his first day. I have to admit that what we did was fucking dreadful. This was the job that was dramatised in *Take It Or Leave It*: it was comical, there was no way we were going to get away with it. The wall had lumps in it, fingerprints all over it and bits dripping off. The fella who'd given us the job showed up and you can imagine the look on his face when he saw it.

I went on the defensive and did my best to convince the fella that everything was in hand, it was all simply part of the process. Suggs ambled over to the window and was trying his best to hide his laughter, as he listened to my rantings about being a qualified plasterer. Of course, the fella wasn't having any of it. We were asked to put down our trowels and fuck off.

I remember getting into the van and saying to Suggs, "What a fucking idiot he was!" I really did believe I was a qualified plasterer after being in that game for two months.

Outside of band rehearsals and work, Debbie and I were going strong. It would be a few more years until we got married. Before then, we'd also get away on a few holidays. Our first was down at Leysdown on the Isle of Sheppey, Kent, with Chris and his partner Sue. It was a caravanning holiday and at the time Leysdown was a hot spot, very popular with Londoners. I recall that the weather wasn't brilliant, so we spent most of the holiday either in the pub or the amusement arcades.

I was coming out of that unsettled period where I'd been squatting and travelling back and forth from Luton. I'd tried my hand at all sorts of jobs and the band was starting to take things seriously, playing on a regular basis and building a fan base; 2Tone had also entered our lives.

I believe that Suggs and Mike went to see The Specials at the Hope & Anchor, then afterwards Suggs and Jerry Dammers went off for a drink together. I wasn't there so I only found out afterwards, but I know Suggs was made up that there was another band playing the same kind of music as us, who even dressed like us. I think Jerry ended up staying with Suggs because he didn't have any digs of his own. I can only imagine they sat up drinking and talking about our two bands.

Horace Panter: The first time I met Lee was when The Specials were playing at the Hope & Anchor. Lee, looking quite nervous, came up to me and asked me if I could help him. He told me that Madness were on the verge of getting a publishing deal and professed that he had no idea about such matters. The thing was that neither did I. He then told me that the band were going to Liverpool and he was trying to find out what it would be like, would it be okay playing there? His perception of gong north of Watford was quite funny. The thing was that six months later, they were headlining shows in other countries.

I remember looking at Madness and thinking they were like a 'firm' on tour. They had people like the brother of Chas Smash and Harry Wandsworth, who sold all the merchandise. When it came to things like that, Madness really had their eye on the ball. They sold t-shirts like nobody's business and we had no t-shirts at all. Madness learned about the business as well as their craft on stage.

From first meeting Lee and Madness and them and us getting records out, things seemed to happen very fast. The Specials had already been playing for a couple of years and had toured with bands like The Clash, but for Madness it had only really been a few months. They'd probably only played as far south as Brixton.

I don't think Jerry had actually set up 2Tone at this stage, but he was in the process of putting the label together. I think he'd already had talks with Chrysalis Records, who were well established and had put out bands like Generation X. I imagine they saw the potential for British ska music with that punk twist.

Even in the early stages, Jerry had all the vision and ambition for 2Tone. All that black-and-white stuff was already in his head, he just needed more bands than The Specials to be part of it.

Horace Panter: Discovering that there was a band doing something similar to us was great, we didn't feel threatened by it at all. We saw Lee and the band as being the same, but different. They didn't have the funk that The Specials had, or that rock'n'roll edge, but they had the pop element which they did very well and it suited them. Terry [Hall] described it as "healthy rivalry".

Madness were in the right place at the right time. 'The Prince' was a perfect song for 2Tone. What we liked was that Madness didn't sound like The Specials, they complemented us. It was obvious that they referenced the same sound and styles of music as us, and it worked for them as it did us. But whereas The Specials sounded like we were more influenced by The Clash, Madness sounded like they looked to a band like The Kinks and those storytelling bands of the previous era.

Debbie: I went to see The Specials at the Hope & Anchor but I had no idea what to expect, I hadn't even heard of them. When I saw them I just thought, 'Oh my God!' It was very weird seeing another band who played music like Madness and looked like Madness. I really did think The Specials were great and it was clear they and Madness were going in the same direction. It was a natural progression for Madness to be signed to 2Tone.

Harry Wandsworth: I was at the gig at the Nashville when Madness and The Specials played on the same night. This was the first time I saw Madness. I'd actually gone to see The Specials, because I'd heard them on the radio. I always got to venues early enough to catch the support bands and that night it was Madness. I can vividly remember Carl doing his 'Hey you!' and his dancing, and it just blew my mind.

And then there was Lee, who was also amazing to watch. It was clear that he had an important part to play too in the live show. I think this gig was the one where Madness had to shoot off to play another one at the Dublin Castle.

It was a few weeks later when I saw Madness again. That was when Carl threw his porkpie hat into the audience and I managed to grab it. After the band played, I bowled into their changing room and that was the first time I spoke to Lee. He and I became friends; he was always happy to make friends with people, always willing to talk to people that came to see the band.

(I'd even end up living at his house that he'd buy in Fairbridge Road, just off of the Holloway Road near Archway. A few of us stayed in Lee's place, including two scousers called Ian and Dave. At times it was quite chaotic.)

I then went to see Madness in a pub called the Pied Bull at the Angel, Islington. There were quite a lot of youngsters in there, myself included. At some point in the night the police came to see if there were any underage drinkers in the pub. A load of us spotted them and bundled into the toilets. We hid for a few minutes but the police didn't check for us in there. But then the door opened and Suggs threw in a handful of lollipops, yelling, "You can all come out of the bogs now!"

I remember going to meet The Specials when they came back to London to play at the Nashville and we all talked about the record label then. We actually supported them that night and this all came about after Suggs and Jerry had first met.

John Hasler: I was managing Madness at the time they did 'The Prince' with 2Tone but wasn't involved with it. Suggs had conversations with Jerry [Dammers] and that's just what it was: Jerry saying that he had a record label and he needed some bands to sign to it. It wasn't me, but someone sent Jerry the demo recording of 'The Prince' and as soon as he heard it he had no hesitation, he wanted to put the record out.

Jerry's offer to have a record put out on his label did come out of the blue. We were also still fairly new to this music-business game. Madness needed a song that was suited to 2Tone. That was how 'The Prince' came about: I got my head down, drew on one of my ska idols, Prince Buster, and came up with the song – which was presented to the band and then eventually to Jerry.

Chalky: I'm not even sure Madness ever signed a contract with Jerry Dammers and 2Tone. I know the deal was for only one record, so this meant that after 'The Prince' they needed a new record company. I remember being with Suggsy and on a couple occasions with Lee, phoning up record labels and telling them that we needed a deal. They'd get all excited and invite us down for lunch and meetings. We'd go and meet with these people at their offices and whilst there, Lee would write our names and addresses in their mail-out book. It was their system for sending out records to DJs and journalists. Once our names were in their books, we'd be sent loads of records on a weekly basis. Most of the records were crap and we'd end up selling them on.

Lee was really good at sniffing out opportunities like that. He puts on this mask of being the Keith Moon of the saxophone, but his eyes were always wide open to opportunities and to what people were doing. He learned about all the record companies' tricks and sussed them out early on. He's much more astute than what he likes people to think.

Neville Staple: I thought 'The Prince' was a great song, and I thought the idea of writing a song about Prince Buster was a great idea too. That song still stands up today. But then Lee is a good songwriter.

Debbie: I remember Lee told me that he'd written a song called 'The Prince'. When he told me what the song was about, I thought, 'What a brilliant idea.' No one had done a tribute song about Prince Buster. It sort of developed from them playing it at their rehearsals. He was really chuffed that the band chose 'The Prince' to record and even more chuffed when they agreed it should be released as a single.

Lynn Milsom: By the time 'The Prince' came out we could see that Madness were in a different league to most of the bands around them. They were polished and looked so slick. It was clear that they had *something*. One of the things I loved about Lee was that he was always coming up with amazing ideas. I was so proud when 'The Prince' was released. It was the beginning of something special for Madness – a new era!

Chalky: 'The Prince' was a unique Madness song. They did really well with their musicianship abilities at that time. It had only been a few months earlier when they were still playing covers like 'The Tears Of A Clown'. But 'The Prince' was the opportunity for each Madness band member to come through, and they did. I think it gave Madness their presence.

The recording they did on an eight-track was never intended to be released as a record, it was only meant for publishing purposes. It was Jerry Dammers who told them that was the version they should release and he put it out on 2Tone. I remember Jerry saying that when he was on his way with Suggs and me to *Top Of The Pops* in an old Morris Minor.

When we got there, we parked up beside this huge artic lorry. It turned out to be the equipment of The Crusaders, who were on tour in the UK. They had stacks of equipment and there was us turning up with a couple of guitars. But in what seemed like no time at all we found ourselves in the charts, driving around in bigger vehicles and carrying around a lot more equipment too.

Amidst all of this, some members of Madness and our producer, Clive Langer, went to see Rob Dickins at Warner Bros Music. He gave us a publishing advance of £150, to cover the songs we'd record during a day session at Pathway Studios. The studios were located at Newington Green and it was there that The Damned had recorded 'New Rose'. (Bands like The Police and Dire Straits also used Pathway.) It was also there that we'd later film some scenes for *Take It Or Leave It*.

The studio was booked and we were all excited about it. I drove there in my Morris van and Mike in his. Woody chose to follow us on his motorbike but en route we managed to lose him. All the rest of the band got to Pathway okay and unloaded our equipment. I carried my sax under one arm and under the other was Woody's bag, with some drumsticks and a half-eaten nut loaf.

We set up. But Woody never showed up and we had no way of contacting him. We couldn't go ahead and record without our drummer, so the session was buggered. It was our first recording session and we fucked it up. To this day I don't know where Woody ended up, but none of us were best pleased with him.

I'd been very excited during the build-up to our first recording session. The thought of walking away from the studio with a recorded song was unbelievable. After our initial balls-up, we did manage to get back into the studio and record 'The Prince'. It was during that recording that I first heard myself really play. Once I put those headphones on it was like *wow!*

John Hasler: I think 'The Prince' is a small masterpiece. I was in the studio when they recorded it and so I saw it come together. I remember they had issues sorting Chrissy's guitar strings out. They were trying to get a certain sound and hit certain notes. Chris could play it live without any problems, but in the studio he was hitting strings he shouldn't. In the end, Clive Langer suggested it would be best to put some gaffer tape over the bottom four strings.

In the studio they played 'The Prince' as a band. There was very little messing around with overdubs. It was kept raw because at the time it was laid down as a demo. It wasn't meant to be the final recording. Neither was it intended to be a single. I think there was even some hesitation from Mike to allow it to be released on a record.

Once it did come out, they all loved it. They then re-recorded 'The Prince'. This was unusual but after 2 Tone they signed to Stiff Records and the album came out. That's probably why they had to re-record it – so that Stiff owned a recording of the song too.

When 2 Tone put 'The Prince' out I got the credit as the writer. I felt incredibly proud, but I was fully aware that it was a Madness song and we had all contributed to it. We recorded 'Madness' itself as the B-side too. (Once we'd signed to Stiff Records we'd re-record 'The Prince' so that version could be used for the *One Step Beyond…* album. 'Madness' was also re-recorded and included on the album, but as a secret track. It wasn't listed on the sleeve.)

'My Girl' also got recorded in that initial session with Mike on vocals. It didn't do the song justice though so it was redone with Suggs. Clive Langer was present during those sessions and he would stay with Madness for a long time. But our recordings were pretty raw and without a lot of overdubs. We caught our sound of that period.

I didn't hear 'The Prince' again for a while. After the recording session the tape was taken to the record company. The first time I saw the record was when John Hasler presented it to me, just before we were about to head up north for a gig. John had a copy for each band member, which he handed out with a huge grin on his face. It was a very special moment.

I held in my hand the seven-inch of one of my songs, recorded with my mates in our band. I'd grown up with records and they were so important to my generation. I could never have imagined, when I played on the grass outside of Denyer House, that one day I'd actually make one. The feeling was amazing.

John Hasler: When I was the Madness manager, I had offices in the same building as Rick Rogers who was managing The Specials during that period. Madness were waiting with the tour bus at The Roundhouse and I was in the offices waiting for a delivery of a box of 'The Prince'. Those offices were the hub of 2Tone at the time and that's where the records came into.

I remember time was getting on and the records hadn't arrived. There was a risk that the band would have to get on the bus and leave, without seeing them. But then they did arrive; I grabbed them off of the delivery driver and legged it up to The Roundhouse.

I handed out the records to Lee and the band and I could see in his eyes that he was really made up. It wasn't like he was jumping about, but you could see him looking at it and thinking, 'Yeah.' It must have been really something for him to actually hold a record of a song he'd written.

Everyone was pleased to get their records. They wanted extra copies to give to their family and friends. They were genuinely excited but there wasn't a conversation about selling loads of records. Having a hit wasn't on their minds. They just felt great to have a record out. They felt proud. We all did.

Just having 'The Prince' committed to vinyl was enough. It didn't matter if it became a hit or not. The added advantage was that our song was on the 2 Tone label: it looked fantastic all in black and white, with Walt Jabsco standing proud. We were fortunate to be on the label at the time when they released their records with the logo on the paper sleeves, because later 2 Tone releases didn't include it.

Toks: When 'The Prince' came out, I was chuffed for them. I mean, my mates putting a record out. I was pleased I had mates that were in a band, but I'd never wanted to. I was happy just going to see them. Madness had come out of punk and punk had told people that they could do it. 'The Prince' was confirmation of that. Being part of 2 Tone was great too, as was getting to know The Specials. We all got on really well.

'Gangsters' by The Special AKA was serial number TT1, 'The Selecter' by The Selecter was TT2 and 'The Prince' was the label's third release, issued as CHS TT3. I've still got the copy that John gave me. The sleeve is signed by the other Madness band members and even some of the road crew. Prince Nutty also got to scribble his name on it.

Neville Staple: Before The Specials started playing in London, I had no idea there was this other band who also played the same sort of music as us and who wore the same style of clothes. But when I saw Madness I liked that they had their own interpretation of ska. I felt that what they were doing worked. I also thought it was a good thing when Madness came onto 2Tone. We got other bands involved too, like Dexys Midnight Runners. I don't think any of us in The Specials were like, 'Oh God, who are this lot?' No, we were all fine with it.

Harry Wandsworth: Madness played a handful of dates as a warm-up to the 2Tone Tour. I bunked off of school to go and see them. For one of the gigs they supported the Merton Parkas at Nottingham University, and I remember that was the night when I really focused on Lee. He had some kind of trampoline and used to bounce up and down and off; it was very funny to watch.

I was very much into dancing by then and had learned all the moves that Carl and Suggs did. The band actually got me up on stage that night, and I danced beside Carl and Suggs. I even ended sleeping in Suggs' bed that night – I don't know where Suggs ended up.

Debbie: One night Lee, Suggs and me went with Jerry Dammers to some flat in Chalk Farm. He had 'Ne-Ne Na-Na Na-Na Nu-Nu' by Bad Manners and kept playing it over and over again. He must have played it ten times. Lee, Suggs and me were just sat there laughing our heads off. Amidst all the laughter, Jerry was talking to Lee and Suggs about Madness going on the 2 Tone Tour with The Specials. It sounded like a great idea.

I went to most of the gigs on the 2 Tone Tour and loved it. Seeing the bands play at that time was incredible. The people in the crowds loved it too. It didn't matter to them which band played first or last, they jumped up and down for three solid hours and were happy to be part of the 2 Tone thing. All the bands on the tour seemed equal, there was no suggestion that one was better or more successful than the other. That's what made it special.

Now that Madness were a 2 Tone band, we were invited to be part of their tour. Madness and the other bands met up outside The Roundhouse in Chalk Farm. We all climbed onto the coach and charged forward towards the seat of our choosing. I plonked down in mine and got comfortable. In just a few minutes the coach was packed full. I looked around at all the excitable faces. It was like the school trips to the seaside that we'd never had.

However, what struck me was that there was only one female amongst us, which was Pauline Black of The Selecter. My initial thought was, 'Oh, there's that singer from The Selecter.' My second thought was, 'Blimey, she must have some balls getting on this coach with us lot!' Pauline held her own though. I found her to be friendly, nice and very quiet. She'd checked me, and kept me at a distance for the whole tour!

Suggs tells a story that, on the first day of the tour, he and some others from The Selecter and The Specials got into an altercation with the Old Bill at a service station. This was even before we'd played a single note. I can't recall when it happened, but it seems pretty clear in Suggs' mind.

Neville Staple: We got Madness onto the 2Tone Tour. There was some trouble on the first day. There were always going to be some problems because I was a proper rude boy back in them days. There were so many incidents on that tour it's hard to pick out one, but there was some bother that Suggs and me got into with some police on the first day. We were all just kids at the time. We just wanted to have fun and enjoy life.

Travelling on the tour bus with all the other band members was a lot of fun. We were all like a big bunch of friends coming together (although not everyone got on). We kept ourselves amused and I can't deny there was a cloud of haze at the back of the bus. I do remember we had a lot of fun on that tour.

I also recall getting on really well with Lee. We had a special connection. He could have been any of my school friends who I'd grown up with. Lee and me are the ones that get the buzz going. We're performers. When I was on stage with The Specials I was the one who jumped around and climbed up things, and that was exactly what Lee did when he was on stage with Madness. We got the fun going.

I enjoyed seeing Lee on stage back in 1979 and I still do. He's done some stuff with my wife Christine at Skamouth* and all these years later, we still get on like

---

* The Great Yarmouth ska weekender.

we always did. He's as down to earth as he always was and he's continued to write brilliant songs.

I got on with all the members of The Selecter: Pauline, Arthur, Neol, Charley H., Charley A. and Desmond. I think Desmond took a disliking to Chrissy Boy, but I'm not sure why. I'm sure they got around it though. (I can't remember if it was before Chris got him in a headlock or after. There's a photograph of that incident.)

Someone we all needed by our side on the coach was Steve English. He was our security guy and he really knew his stuff. He also knew how to open a venue's exit door with troublesome people's heads, when required.

So the coach set off for where we were booked to play the first night, at the Brighton Top Rank. There are some amazing photographs of us all on the famous pebble beach. Most of us are plonked down on the pebbles, dark glasses and Harrington jackets on, though there are several white socks on show too. *Oh dear!*

Following Brighton, the next town on the 2Tone Tour was Swindon; from there we travelled to Bournemouth and then on to Exeter. It was an assault on the southwest coastline. We then went north towards Birmingham and Blackburn, Leicester and other towns before dropping back down to Portsmouth and bouncing back up to Cardiff and then hitting Newcastle.

Madness opened with 'Tarzan's Nuts' and ended with 'The Prince'. The tour was a success, but we actually jumped off early because we needed to go to America. Dexys Midnight Runners replaced us and finished the tour, but not before we invaded the stage, along with The Selecter, to join The Specials for a knees-up to 'Skinhead Moonstomp'. It would inevitably end up with loads of kids getting on stage too and having a good stomp in their DMs.

I only have fond memories of that tour. It never got boring for me. I totally enjoyed it. Madness had toured before, so we had some idea what to expect, but we weren't prepared for the fantastic response that we got. The whole 2Tone movement was in full swing and we were part of it. We were making history.

The after-show parties on the 2Tone Tour were legendary. It was great on so many levels because we were all young, excited, creative and up for it. Our audiences were also young, excited and up for it. We were all out to have fun and, at that time, all of us got on. There were a lot of laughs. There was a lot of alcohol consumed too.

We would return to most, if not all, of the venues that Madness played on that tour in the years after. Things would be different, the audiences were different, we wore different clothes, as did our audiences, and we'd have loads of new songs. But the 2Tone Tour was a little piece of magic that happened at the right time, with the right people, the right music and the right fashion. It was never designed to last because things change and move on, and that's okay.

A film called *Dance Craze* immortalised Madness and the other bands on the 2Tone Tour (including some bands who weren't signed to 2Tone, like Bad Manners). As with *Quadrophenia*, I haven't seen the film since I first saw it (back in 1981).

But I went to the premiere. I even got taken there in a Rolls-Royce which belonged to Alan Winstanley, Clive Langer's production partner. I was dressed to the nines, not in a Ben Sherman, Levi's and DMs but in a dinner suit with a dickie-bow. As we drove through the streets on our way, I remember we threw eggs out of the Roller and yelled out, "Down with capitalism!" It seemed like a fun thing to do at the time.

I don't really recall what I thought of *Dance Craze*, but it certainly seemed to capture the chaos and vibrancy of the gigs from that period. That whole 2Tone Tour, our connection with the label and the other bands all seemed to happen so fast. I'm still grateful for 2Tone helping to put Madness on the map. I also made friendships that have lasted forty years. All these years later, some of those people still tell me how much they loved that 2Tone period that peaked in 1980, culminating in the classic Specials number one 'Ghost Town' in 1981.

The 2Tone UK tour started off in Brighton in October 1979 and finished several weeks later in November. Madness left early to tour the East and West Coasts of the USA, performing in clubs like Hurrah and Mudd Club in NYC, as well as the Whisky A Go Go in LA.

Dexys Midnight Runners replaced us on the final leg of the 2Tone Tour. There was a definite change of mood on the tour bus after this, as Dexys had a different image they wanted to portray, i.e. moody, tight unit, professional. Madness had been a bunch of out-of-control, pissed-up, disruptive fuckers on a school trip. As much as The Selecter's Pauline Black found us entertaining, I reckon she was pleased to see the back of us!

Harry Wandsworth: Before Madness got a tour bus they were driven around in a van. I got on that a few times. I was in the back one night when Chalky, Toks and Tony Duffield [the Madness tour manager] were driving. I was huddled in one of the corners of the van, amongst all the equipment. It was freezing, so they told me to get up front with them.

That night a roadie saved my life, because there was an accident. I'd dropped off but was awoken by the sound of a massive bang. Something had hit the van and what's more, the area that was damaged the worst was where I'd originally tried to put my head down.

Being in that accident didn't put me off travelling with Madness though. I did a lot of the 2Tone Tour but I had to get by Steve English, who was the bands' security. One night, Lee got me onto the coach but Steve spotted me and told him I couldn't be there because I wasn't part of the band or its crew. Lee said okay, sorry, and I got off – but he had no intention of letting me down, so he sneaked me back onto the coach and I crouched down between some seats, out of Steve's view.

I stayed there for the entire journey until we reached the next destination. As I ambled off of the coach, Steve saw me and said, "You little fucker!", waving me on. But that was Lee, if he could help you out he would.

Hearing 'The Prince' on the radio for the first time was another magical moment. I was actually painting an old cast-iron bed frame at the time. I'd picked up some work from an old lady because I still needed to bring some kind of wage in. I had a small transistor radio on as I painted away and, suddenly, 'The Prince' came on.

Radio 1, the most popular radio station in the country, was playing our song. *Wow!* The DJ was Paul Burnett, whom I would listen to religiously in the 70s (his voice was humorous, unpretentious and made me smile), before Steve Wright took his seat.

Debbie: When I heard 'The Prince', I thought it was great. I still do. There's so much that goes in just a couple of minutes. At the time of the record coming out, I was working in a factory that made spectacles. We listened to a radio as we worked and suddenly the presenter announced that a song called 'The Prince' by Madness had gone into the charts (at whatever number) and the whole factory gave a huge cheer. It was a really emotional moment and one that I'll never forget. Hearing a song that Lee had written on the radio, and hearing that it had got into the top forty, was amazing. The charts were very important to us back then, everybody paid attention to them. I felt very proud of what Lee and the band had accomplished.

It's a strange feeling hearing your record on the radio for the first time. There are lots of different emotions and thoughts racing through your head. I remember feeling something a bit similar when I first heard 'What A Waste' – I felt kind of proud because I'd been going see Ian Dury and his band since the Kilburn and the High Roads days. Hearing his record being played on the radio was like, 'Yeah, you've arrived!'

Tracy: I thought 'The Prince' was brilliant and was shocked that it didn't go to number one. I thought the song was that good and the idea of it being about Prince Buster was fantastic.

Lee was into his black music. There were times when he'd ask me questions about black culture and the meaning of the words they used. I had some knowledge because I'd go out with black fellas. Lee was curious and wanted to understand the culture from where ska music had come, so I'd tell him what this or that word meant and how to pronounce it – things like 'bredren'.

I felt so proud of Lee when he handed me a copy of 'The Prince'. He was good like that, he'd always get me copies of their records as they got released. We were all really proud of him: Mum and Dad, the family.

I went along with the rest of the band to Holts in Camden, where The Specials had their offices located above the shop. We were all suited and booted because it was looking like we might be getting on *Top Of The Pops*. However, the news filtered through that we wouldn't be getting the invite because Secret Affair's record had sold better that week, so they got to go on the show instead of us. I was truly gutted. But then 'The Prince' sold well the following week and we got the invite.

John Hasler: I was with the band when they went down to *Top Of The Pops* for their first appearance and it was absolute chaos. It's amazing how they ever got invited back. The BBC was a very tightly run ship and Madness weren't going to fit smoothly into that. It must have been a bit awkward for Woody because his parents worked for *Top Of The Pops*. His dad was a photographer on the show.

On the day they were a bit difficult to control. There was a fair bit of them walking around the corridors and finding themselves in areas that they shouldn't be in. There were a lot of BBC people saying stuff like, "Who are you? What are you doing here? You can't be in here!" I got quite a few complaints that day. They were even told they weren't allowed to go into the 'famous' BBC bar, but they blagged their way in somehow.

Once they were on *Top Of The Pops* they felt like they were the dog's bollocks. To be invited on the show meant that their record had sold well. It was like having the official confirmation that 'The Prince' was a hit.

Top Of The Pops wasn't a live show. It was all recorded a day or two before it got broadcast on Thursday. When we went along (after the false alarm care of Secret Affair, who had nicked our slot the previous week), for ease of carting a saxophone around with me, I took along a plastic toy saxophone and pretended to play that while we were filmed. I happily mimed along to 'The Prince'. I was in my element.

When we were invited back to be filmed again, this time I took along a baritone saxophone. That was the one that later got stolen from my flat in the Caledonian Road. I'm not sure what the more astute viewer must have thought when they saw me playing that little toy one week and a massive sax the next, but it was brilliant to perform on *Top Of The Pops* twice. A coup, but this novelty would in time soon tire as producer Michael Hurll was not happy to have us fucking around on his watch. But it confirmed the song was doing well – it would get to number sixteen and spend eleven weeks in the charts.

Horace Panter: I heard that Lee actually learned to play the saxophone wrong and that was down to the way it was tuned. I like that story. I mean how punk is that?

For me, Lee very quickly created a sense of the bizarre, which I thought was fantastic. It was as if he didn't take it all too seriously. He did ridiculous things like appear on *Top Of The Pops* with a plastic saxophone, or he'd wear a huge U-boat captain's coat. But he'd manage to make it work, whereas most people would just look silly. He has that ability to take the piss out of himself. It was as if he saw Madness having some success but he didn't know how long it would last, so he decided to just have as much fun as possible.

Chalky: It was a bit bizarre when 'The Prince' got released. At times it felt a bit odd. We were suddenly popping around the corner to White City to go and do *Top Of The Pops*. We went from our familiar surroundings to these big establishments.

A few years ago, Madness played on the roof of Buckingham Palace. I sent Lee a text saying, 'Get down from there before they find out.' That's what it felt like when they started going on *Top Of The Pops*. It was as if they were going to be found out at any moment. Whatever they did, it still felt like we were gate-crashing parties back in Hampstead. It felt like we shouldn't really be invited, but we were going to get inside and have a go anyway.

Debbie: When I saw Madness perform 'The Prince' on *Top Of The Pops* my first thought was, 'Why is Lee playing a silly toy saxophone?' I had no idea he was going to do that. I don't even know if he'd told the band. I pulled him about it afterwards though, saying, "Why can't you be more serious?" But that was Lee, that's the kind of thing he would do.

John Hasler: After 'The Prince' came out the crowds at gigs got bigger. By the time the record came out they were already packing out places like the Dublin Castle and when they played 'The Prince', they got a good reaction from the audience. This continued, but with something extra – the cheers were louder.

Because we had a top-twenty hit Madness became flavour of the month. Our agreement with 2Tone was for just one single, so we were being shopped around other labels. Several record labels met with us, wining and dining us in an attempt to sign us up.

Harry Wandsworth: There was a punk band called The Straps. At the time when they were going, I was also doing a lot of graffiti, writing up stuff like 'Wandsworth Harry the Madness Nutter'. I wrote that everywhere, and one of those was on a wall where The Straps had written up some stuff too. There was no problem until the day after Madness had been on *Top Of The Pops*. I walked past the wall and happened to notice they'd written 'wankers' underneath 'Madness'. But I was okay with it because it sort of confirmed to me that Madness had made it. As far as I know, The Straps never got a record deal – wankers!

We had a hit record and record labels were hungry for us. My family and friends were happy for me and the band. My dad wrote me a letter, which I still possess to this day. It was sent from Her Majesty's Prison Norwich (his residence at the time).

In my dad's letter, he offers his advice on what he thinks is best regarding signing new contracts. His main point was 'keep it short, never sign a long-term deal,' explaining that The Beatles only signed contracts with a short timescale.

I took his advice and even today, I never sign up to long deals. My mobile phone contracts are always short ones. My BT one ends soon and I can't wait to get out of it...

My mum was pleased for me too and had her own advice. Her main concern was the 'rock'n'roll' lifestyle' that she thought she knew all about. Her generation had witnessed Paul McCartney publicly talking about taking LSD and there had been a lot of media coverage when Mick Jagger and Keith Richards got arrested for drugs. There had also been popstar deaths: Jimi Hendrix, Brian Jones, Jim Morrison and Janis Joplin. My mum's advice was, "Don't do drugs and bank your money." She was just being protective, like a mother should be.

Despite having a record out and being on *Top Of The Pops*, I carried on just being me. My family treated me the same. If anything, I noticed more of a change in some of my mates, but I don't think I walked into my local pub full of ego – ya know, Billy big bollocks. I'd known these people since my schooldays and they knew exactly who I was or what I wasn't. Which some say involved squeaking when walking.

I can't deny I liked the praise when people showed their appreciation of 'The Prince'. When it came down to it though, I was still that Aldenham Youth Club oik who liked to climb up lampposts and break into telephone boxes for a few coins.

Funnily enough, I get more tongue-in-cheek jokes from my mates now. My pal Pat often pulls out the "Have you got a spare ticket for your old mate who's living in a cardboard box?" He always gets the same reply: "Pat, I would, but I'm down to my last two million."

The topic of money can often be an awkward one. I suppose some people did think that once 'The Prince' came out, we were playing better gigs and getting ourselves on the telly, we were rolling in money. I did get a royalty from 'The Prince' but I can't say for what amount. It would have been absorbed by everything else going on at the time.

But I do remember getting my first cheque after signing to Stiff Records. It was for £1,000. I still have the bank statement. Each member of Madness got the same amount. A grand was a lot of money in 1979: the average annual wage was around £5,000 and you could buy a house for twenty thousand.

Horace Panter: I remember when Madness were just about to go on their first tour of America. Their manager at the time needed them to fill in some forms, before they could apply for their visas. The form included a section where they had to disclose if they'd ever had any trouble with the law. You could almost see the manager's jaw drop as he read down the list that Lee had written.

12

Calling Cards

By 1979 the next wave of mods and skinheads was picking up momentum, along with the rude boys. It was a decade after the original mod and skinhead scenes, so it was a revival – although many people didn't like that term.

All the same, I saw kids in our audiences and in the streets that wore some nice clothes, just like I had back in the late 1960s. It was good to see lads raid their older brothers' wardrobes, brush off the moths and put on a tailor-made, three-button tonic suit with a ticket pocket.

I'd always liked a nice suit. There was a time when I was searching thrift stores for 1940s zoot suits and similar. The zoot style had been adopted by the teddy boys in the 1950s in their supposedly Edwardian drape jackets. Jazz musicians like Cab Calloway made them popular in the 1940s, as did Tom and Jerry in *The Zoot Cat*.

Malcolm X described the zoot as "a killer-diller coat with a drape shape". I really liked the cut of the trousers too.

They were high-waisted, wide-legged and pegged. David Bowie was a lover of zoot suits and was photographed wearing them numerous times. Mike, Chris and me liked the zoot suit because we were really into that whole 1940s American look. There was something very stylish about the era.

The look was made for people of my stature, i.e. rounded biceps, firm pecs, short legs and deep pockets. As I was little in leg the trousers were cut high, almost coming up to the bottom of the nipple area when worn with wishbone braces – thereby giving the illusion my legs were very long, as if you were in a house of mirrors. These suits would set the dancefloor alight when worn with a pair of Allen Edmonds American brogues, box tie and silver tie-clip, trilby and a splash of Henry Cooper's Brut.

There was a shop just by the Finchley Road & Frognal train station that sold zoot suits. (It's long gone now, just a part of the London Overground.) We'd often pop into that shop when visiting a car-breaker's yard just a short walk away. We needed to make one such visit following an incident in Mike's car.

I jumped in it following one of our rehearsals and we set off. We hadn't been on the road too long when out of the blue some fella simply wandered into the road on Rosslyn Hill, Hampstead. The car went smack into him and he went down, leaving a smidge of snot and sweat on the windscreen. Mike stopped the car and we looked at each other. We couldn't believe what had happened. But then we saw fingers appearing on the bonnet and this figure rising up. He didn't even look at us, just shuffled off instead.

Mike was cursing him. "What an idiot, he didn't even look!" We hadn't gone far before he pulled over again and leapt out of the car.

"Bloody hell! My headlight's been knocked out!" He then decided to do something about it, running back up the hill to find the fella to get some cash out of him for a new light.

We went to that breaker's yard to get a new headlight. We'd go there several times, looking for replacement parts for our Morris vans – though not because we'd run down any daydreamers, thankfully! It was a fascinating place, with the various models of cars stacked up on top of one another, those crash-and-bashed-up old 60s English models that wore the American influence on a much tinier scale. But it's long gone. Now it's office space with a Starbucks on top of it.

Back to the suits...

I liked seeing kids starting to look stylish, even though they put their own spin on it. They had to, as it wasn't 1964 or 1969 anymore.

When Madness got going and the 2Tone bands were breaking through, there was the rude-boy look too. Horace Panter and Jerry Dammers worked with a couple of graphic designers to come up with the black-and-white 2Tone logo: a rude boy they named Walt Jabsco, in a black suit, white shirt, white socks and loafers. That defined the rude-boy look of the late 1970s. It wasn't so much the look that the Jamaican diaspora had introduced into Britain in the previous decade, as Walt was inspired by a photograph Dammers and Panter had seen of Peter Tosh.

I first noticed the rude boys at The Specials' 1979 gig at the Nashville Rooms. At first I thought they were Jam fans, because Weller, Foxton and Buckler wore black suits with white shirts and black ties. It was their look in 1977 when 'In The City' came out. But these kids I saw dancing along to The Specials looked good – all bar the white socks.

I cannot stand white socks. In fact, such is my disdain that I walked into the Alexandra pub in High Barnet once and, being a bit pissed, yelled, "Is anyone wearing white socks?" About a dozen blokes shouted back, "Yeah!" "Right," I continued, "well, take them off!" They did. I gathered them up and tossed them into the fire.

My friend Lofty didn't believe I'd do it. But it wasn't so much the smoke that was a problem, it was more the pong from the nylon socks. It was a relief that the manager was understanding, on the whole...

I just never liked that look of white socks on display beneath a pair of Sta-Prest, or poking out from a nice pair of brogues or loafers. It was so common at the end of the 1970s but I detested it. However, I did love a pair of luminous socks, which also got quite popular for a period of time.

Socks had always been an important part of a look. I'd first caught on to it when the suedehead thing came in: yellow, red, blue or mustard socks were essential.* I remember going to school one day feeling like the dog's bollocks in a pair of

---

* I pulled a suit out of my wardrobe recently made by Frank Rossi, who still has a shop on Fortess Road in Kentish Town. He made some of the suits Madness wore for their promo videos. It had some socks with it which reminded me of the colourful ones I used to buy from his shop all those years ago.

dogtooth trousers, polished brogues and bright, brand-new red socks. The headmaster called me into the office and I was expecting a telling off for my strides. But it was my red socks he didn't like and I got sent home.

The mod and skinhead looks, along with the emergence of the rude boy, were what British kids were into when 'One Step Beyond...' got released. I don't know if the rude-boy thing was more popular in the Midlands because of The Specials coming out of Coventry, but I don't recall it being as big in London. It may have been that I didn't notice it as much in the places I knocked around, as my mates were more into the skinhead look.

There were also people I would see around places like Camden that took elements of the skinhead look I'd known but added their own parts to it. Whereas I'd worn Dr Martens with a few extra inch boot holes added, there were now skinheads bowling around in twenty-hole boots. Seemed a little bit S&M to me, but each to their own.

That late 1970s skinhead look was more aggressive than the 60s version. It also became part of their uniform to have a spider's web tattoo on their neck or a swastika symbol in the middle of their forehead. 'ACAB', meaning 'All Coppers Are Bastards', was quite common on the knuckles, or 'Love' on one hand and 'Hate' on the other. Getting a tattoo hadn't been part of the spirit of '69, and these just weren't that tasteful. Along with the bigger boots and aggressive swagger, it all contributed to giving the movement a lot of negative press.

Not all of them, but sections of the late 70s skinheads got it wrong. Skinhead ranks had always been full of tough, working-class kids, but it was never meant to be thuggish. But then the times probably contributed to the differences. Society and culture had changed a huge amount in ten years: tensions, frictions, conflicts were rife due to the politics of the day and rising unemployment, so I guess people were angrier. We'd seen its influence on punk and I suppose it fuelled the skinhead revival too.

The press had a field day picking on a skinhead who'd been arrested for getting into a fight whilst clinging onto a can of Hurlimann and a bag of glue. Glue sniffing was a drug of choice for many skinheads of that period. It was a horrible thing to do and would often leave some kid covered in spots and scabs, looking just dreadful. Kids would gather under railway arches or bridges, or in parks or graveyards, to do their seedy thing.

I never got the glue-sniffing thing. As far I was aware, it was popular because it was cheap, easily available at all good hardware stores and simple to do. But it was horrible seeing some kid with his face buried in a small plastic bag. It was really dangerous too, especially when mixed with alcohol, and could lead to brain damage. I'm surprised there weren't more horror stories in the news about deaths.

My mates and me swerved anything as stupid as sniffing glue. We preferred to stick to necking blues; you could still function on them into the wee hours at afterhours clubs. They'd been popular amongst the mods in the mid-60s. The characters in *Quadrophenia* are seen popping them throughout the film. (In one scene, some of them break into a chemist's to steal a bottle of blues.)

I remember, whilst doing the gig as Morris and the Minors at the Music Machine, chewing the inside of my mouth out because I'd swallowed a load of blues. I think the whole band had done them too, so it's no surprise we blew Sore Throat off the stage that night.

Blues were obtained in petrol-blue pill form in the mid-70s, then in a bitter, ivory-coloured powder form (sulphate) a few years on. Sulphate was a street drug that I never really took to. It was horrible stuff and a lot of people got into trouble with it – by physically falling in, on and over everything, mainly concrete paving stones. It could be very addictive. But like glue, it was easy to get hold of and cheap.* Like the MDMA and ketamine (special K) of today, it was cheap and as easy to obtain as ordering a pizza. It was lower league – nasty gear.

I don't think the mod revival was that close to the originators either. The music didn't sound anything like the

* Cocaine was on a whole other level and when it was good, it was something else. In the late 1970s and into the 80s, the majority of my cocaine experiences happened outside of the UK, more often than not in America. The first line I ever had was in Los Angeles. It was amazing stuff. It came in small crystal particles but when you chopped it the stuff would fluff up and expand, and the more you chopped it the more it would grow.

I remember being at home on my own with some of that cocaine. I was chopping this stuff up, I thought I was going to end up with a mountain of coke and I was thinking, 'How am I going to explain this away to Debbie?'

But I did my best to shovel my way through it, while a voice in the back of head was whispering, 'I'm never going to touch this stuff again.' Well, of course, that wasn't quite the case – though it's all in the past now and I don't champion it. I've seen too many people get hooked and lose everything because of it. Like all drugs, it should come with a warning. Nowadays, I feel safe and content in my comfort zone with a pint and some pork scratchings. When the fun stops, *stop!*

bands that the mods listened to in the 1960s: Secret Affair, the Merton Parkas and The Lambrettas didn't much resemble the Small Faces, The Who or The Creation to my ears. I think they took more of the originals' dress sense than the music.

The Jam were different though. I felt they stood alone, had their finger on the pulse with their material and were a solid unit. I liked them and their songs a lot, especially their angrier edge. I remember Suggs saw The Jam and got all fired up about them, but some of the other mod bands didn't have a canon of good, original songs.

(I thought the version of 'Poison Ivy' by The Lambrettas was okay. They were on *Top Of The Pops* at the same time as us and Debbie upset one of their members by ruffling up his hair. She'd had a few drinks at the BBC bar.)

> **Toks:** Going along to *Top Of The Pops* was a big deal. The bar was dirt cheap too, so we took advantage of that. We also got to meet a lot of other bands: Sad Café were there on one occasion and I remember having a laugh with them. *Top Of The Pops* was what we all watched and the band were very excited to be on it. They also did *The Old Grey Whistle Test*, which was mainly horrible hippy shit. They did 'Bed And Breakfast Man' on there.

The youth culture in 1979 was mods, skinheads and rude boys, though punks were still around and the soul-boy/girl thing was drawing a crowd. Mod really exploded once *Quadrophenia* was released.

I could relate to the film because I'd seen the original mods running around the place on their scooters and there they were again, buzzing across town. I was curious to see Sting's performance too. He played the Ace Face/bellboy who rides a silver GS Vespa with loads of mirrors on it. Sting was a pop-star-cum-film-star back then and I liked his band, The Police. They had that white reggae thing going on and knew how to write some fantastic two-and-a-half-minute pop tunes.

I thoroughly enjoyed *Quadrophenia*; to me as a twenty-two-year-old, the story, the soundtrack and the cast were all superb. That film kick-started the careers of many of the actors: Philip Davis; Timothy Spall; Ray Winstone; Jesse Birdsall (brother of Simon Birdsall); Phil Daniels, who played the main character, Jimmy Cooper, later appeared in everything from Mike Leigh's *Meantime* to a stint on *EastEnders*. *Quadrophenia* was a complete success on many levels and is still loved and talked about today.*

As a rule, Madness didn't mind the audience being made up of rude boys, skinheads and mods. It was only when things got aggressive and violent, when two tribes had gone to war, that we got pissed off.

There would be nights when we'd have to stop playing and ask the lighting man to point the spotlight at an area of the crowd. What we'd see is half of the room dressed in black-and-white suits pointing at the other half of the room. People dressed in the obligatory 2Tone style were generally there to support the bands. Others, with shaven heads, boots and braces, were most likely to kick off.

---

* At the time of writing this book there were cinemas showing *Quadrophenia* again for its fortieth anniversary. It was also shown on Film 4 in May 2020, during lockdown, and I enjoyed it just as much as in '79 – except for the lengthy adverts in between!

Suggs, Bedders and Chrissy Boy were always the first to witness it, minutes before it was about to go off, as they had a bird's eye view of the movement of potential troublemakers. From previous bundles at Madness concerts, we knew shaming the culprits with the spotlight was the best way to deal with them. The bouncers would then move in to frogmarch them round the back.

Fortunately, this period only lasted for a couple of years before we noticed our audience swelling with new faces. The normal looking 'casual' or market-trader types were neither here nor there – they were along for whatever the evening had to offer.

Once 'My Girl' came out, we started to get a lot more females showing up at our concerts. I suspect they liked the sentiment of that song, plus they'd have seen us on *Top Of The Pops* and known we weren't a bunch of thuggish skinheads out to cause trouble. When we went on *Top Of The Pops* we wore nice white suits and dickie-bows.

Our real turning point would come when 'Embarrassment' was released, in 1980. Our audiences from thereon were a really mixed crowd of mods, skinheads, rude boys, girls and general pop-music fans. It was great to see. The mod/skinhead/rude boy thing didn't really survive that far into the 1980s. It probably had about three or four years when its presence was at full strength, but that was how youth culture worked. It moved on and got replaced by the next new fashion movement.

Madness were able to adapt and move with the times but a lot of other bands were not, or simply didn't want to: 2Tone Records kept going until about 1985, but it wasn't the force it had been between '79 and '81; The Jam got stronger and stronger until Weller broke it up in 1982, to form the Style Council; UB40 evolved into one of the biggest pop acts of the 1980s, but countless other bands with whom we'd shared stages on *Top Of The Pops* split up. I got a record voucher for my 23rd birthday and used it to credibly purchase UB40's debut album, *Signing Off*. It came with a twelve-inch that had 'Reefer Madness' recorded on it; mint track, loads of saucy sax.

The Specials didn't last long past their second album, *More Specials*; by 1984's *In The Studio*, Jerry Dammers had morphed part of the band into the Special AKA. I loved the first album, *The Specials*. I would religiously make my way into the mosh pit and have a ding-dong along to personal favourite 'Blank Expression', often locking eyes with Terry and pointing at each other on the chorus. And, of course, the manic 'Monkey Man' – with Neville going apeshit, firing off a starter pistol into the air – was of its time.

But I *particularly* loved *More Specials*. I'd been hanging around with (Specials guitarist) Roddy Byers at the bar in Dingwalls, talking on the subject of that difficult second album. He asked if I might like to pop by their studio and put a bit of sax on a track he'd written, 'Hey, Little Rich Girl'. I wasn't too sure about taking him up on this as I could get away with my style in Madness – basically out of tune, as can be heard on the recordings. But we were in good spirits, so I went along and put it down in three takes.

Jerry Dammers was at the controls and he didn't mess about! The Special AKA's single release of 'What I Like Most About You (Is Your Girlfriend)' is one of Jerry's masterpieces. I just wish he'd invited me to play along with my old friend

Dick Cuthell (on trumpet). There's a great brass riff at end of the tune and Jerry is wearing a great Bacofoil suit in the video. He looks into the camera, as mad as a box of frogs, and as a spaceship takes off it's like 1950s cinema at its trickiest. And the track is up there with 'Ghost Town' – simple, effective. I'm not sure if I imagined it but I have a vision of drummer Brad (John Bradbury) nailing up some rusty, corrugated iron sheets behind his kit, for that extra *ring-ping-ting* sound!

I got a signed copy in the post shortly before my 23rd birthday, reading 'Congratulations squeaky Lee'.

Terry Hall, Lynval Golding and Neville Staple went on to form the Fun Boy Three, had hits with songs like 'Our Lips Are Sealed' and 'The Lunatics (Have Taken Over The Asylum)' and collaborated with Bananarama on a couple of songs too – all top ten. I was instantly a fan.

We'd also support The Go Go's in the US. Guitarist Jane Wiedlin had a gift for writing a catchy pop tune and they could all cut it live. I'd never get bored with their tunes. They were a laugh, not at all up their own arses and could actually play their instruments. They'd give us a run for our money, in a purely platonic way.*

Neville Staple: My first impressions of Lee were that he was the sort of guy that I could get on with. I can't remember exactly where we first met, but I recall thinking to myself that he was a lot like me. He was outgoing, he was fun to be with and he was someone

---

* Though my wife is convinced I must have banged one or two of them. Seriously.

you wanted to be around. I also found Lee to be down to earth and that was something I could relate to, because that's how I am too.

I've still got the debut Fun Boy Three album at home and I still love it. I was pleased that Terry, Lynval and Neville were able to continue after The Specials. Madness managed to get them into our 'Driving In My Car' video. We're filmed driving down some street in the Shepherd's Bush area in our Morris Maddiemobile, with the MAD 7 number plate, and we pass Terry, Lynval and Neville. Terry is holding up a bit of card with 'Coventry or Not' scribbled on it, as if they're hitchhiking. Of course, we don't stop for them.

It wasn't planned at all. It was only while we were out filming that one of the band spotted them strolling down the street. We asked them if it was okay to film them and they agreed. It all happened as simply as that – though it could have been set up by Robbo (Stiff boss), I dunno.

David Steele and Andy Cox, who had been members of The Beat, another 2Tone band, formed Fine Young Cannibals and members of The Bodysnatchers formed The Belle Stars, who signed to Stiff Records and had huge success with 'The Clapping Song'.

As for Madness, we went from 'The Prince' to 'Our House', 'Wings Of A Dove' and 'Tomorrow's (Just Another Day)' in what seemed like a blink of the eye. The pop world landscape had also changed a lot between 1979 and 1983.

When you think about the bands who were on that 2Tone Tour, Madness were the only group that stuck together. As dysfunctional as we were at times and as much as we could all be unstable – apart from Mark Bedford, who is the most level-headed out of us – somehow we've managed to hold it all together, stay mates, write hit records and draw a good-sized audience. It's been challenging at times but Madness have now celebrated our fortieth anniversary – with a performance at Camden's Electric Ballroom at 1979's entry fee, plus three performances at The Roundhouse back to back, pre-Christmas 2019, titled Madness: Past Present Future.

We're still making music and travelling the world, playing to huge crowds. We've all grown, though we're still pretty much the same people we were back in 1978. When I think of the rows that Mike and I used to have, in particular, the fact that we've managed to remain friends for more than forty years is incredible. Maybe we all need each other. Maybe Madness is much more than just a band to us.

I'm very grateful that it's turned out like this. Madness really has gone from my sitting in launderettes with Mike and Chris, trying to stay warm,* learning to play our instruments, playing in pub basements and releasing our first records to performing on the roof of Buckingham Palace. It's been quite a story!

There are people that have been part of this mad Madness journey that I'm still friends with. Take Chalky and Toks.

---

* It wasn't very hygienic, but I used to cut Mike Barson's and Chrissy Boy's hair in the launderette, with a bladed instrument I'd acquired from Woolworths. You could keep the dryer going by pushing a peg, putting your head in to blow away any itchy hairs and dry yourself off. To get really warmed up, you could place yourself in a dryer, close the door and go for a spin. You'd have to be as mad as a box of frogs to do this, of course!

Those two I consider to have been the rocks of Madness – and no, that's not dyslexia kicking in. They kept it real for us, whilst managing to irritate the management.

Chalky and Toks were our friends, along with John Hasler (and Wandsworth Harry!). They'd been with us since the before the Hope & Anchor days. They were a couple of years younger than me so we didn't really know each other when we were growing up, even though Toks lived just down Highgate Hill from me. My sister and Toks were a couple for a while, but it didn't last.

Chalky and Toks became our roadies. They did what they needed to do to make the band work, despite being a double-act like Statler and Waldorf – the two old moaners on *The Muppet Show*. Their poised, judgmental looks from the wings would bog out the hardest, most egotistical pop stars in the game; especially after coming off when they'd give you marks out of ten. They'd claim to have heard better-played music coming from a kindergarten, or to have witnessed more exciting acts on *The Good Old Days*.

There was nowhere to run or hide on the road. It was a barrage of relentless (mainly verbal) abuse. But Chalky and Toks were our mates, and that's what ultimately mattered. I'd sooner put up with them than be pussyfooted around by some perm-haired, stonewash-clad, key-swinging, gurning, high-kicking, three-bags-full bell-end.

Chalky was one of Suggs' friends and it was Suggs that introduced him to the band. Like Suggs, he was also a Chelsea FC supporter and they'd go to watch their team together. Nowadays he lives in Eastbourne, works with wayward kids and plans to travel around the world in his camper, with his daughter Maisie.

Chalky came along to a Lee Thompson's Ska Orchestra gig in Brighton a little while back and it was really good to see him. But I remember him stepping in and flooring a few blokes at a gig we did in Manchester, when they were giving the band grief. He was useful like that. In fact, he's stuck up for me a few times when I've found myself in a tight spot.

Toks is a really nice fella too, full of qualities. He'd take a bullet for you if he had to. When I was growing up I knew some of the kids he knocked about with, but I didn't get to know him until he started to come to our gigs at the Hope & Anchor. I don't recall Chalky and Toks knowing each other prior to coming to our gigs either. I think Madness was their connection and then they hit it off. When they were on form and rolling – and they always were – they had the best banter and the sharpest wit. You didn't stand a chance.

Toks used to work the door at the Dublin Castle with my wife Debbie. The two of them got on really well together. He then got more and more friendly with the band and Chalky, and it was just a natural progression for them both to end up working as roadies for us.

Toks: I started to turn up at more and more gigs and this led to me helping them carry their gear into the venues. This was how I got involved with working for the band. I'd do some of the driving and I remember going to hire vans that hid the fact that we were from London. This was important because the band were getting gigs up and down the country, and we didn't want people damaging the van.

I have so many good memories from that time. It really was great. It could get a bit wild at times and there were many mornings when I'd wake up and there'd be half a dozen people sleeping in my hotel room. It could be a bit tough too, a bit like going to football matches in the 1970s – we'd carry coshes with us, especially when we went to places like Liverpool and Manchester. We'd expect some aggro and at times there was.

I recall being at Eric's, in Liverpool and Si Birdsall was with us. The promoter had left a few crates of beer in the band's dressing room, so we tucked into that. Si decided to stay in the dressing room and have a kip, while the rest of us went out front to watch the band. Something happened and it all kicked off. Eric's turned into a Wild West saloon, with tables and chairs being smashed. While all this was going on, I remember seeing Si stroll into the room, rubbing his eyes, yawning and wondering what the hell was happening. It was very funny to see.

Chalky: The period from the band getting going to 'The Prince' being released seemed to happen so quickly. It was like one moment they were doing gigs around Camden Town and the next they were playing to big crowds at Eric's in Liverpool. There was a big fight in there, which I still have the scars from. It felt like everywhere we went there was a battle.

It was a bit like football away days. We couldn't just turn up and do the gig. I remember going to Birmingham and having to fight our way out of the Bull Ring. Wherever we went there were people ready to start on us. When we went to places, we'd have to think about our exit plan.

Lee was like a loose cannon on the road. Journeys had to be planned. We had to work out how to get somewhere, how long it would take and what needed to happen at various points on the way. In the early days some of us had jobs to get back for too, so we didn't want to be hanging about in some town up north.

With Lee, you were never sure where he was going to be. There was always an element of keeping you on your toes. When it was sound-checking time, it would be, "Where's Lee?" and someone would tell you he was last seen shopping in town. I was never quite sure if that was code for something else.

With Lee you'd have an initial starting place, but you could guarantee you'd end up somewhere else. It was never straightforward. You couldn't just go from London to Liverpool, you always had to pop in to see so-and-so on the way and they might live a hundred miles off route.

The more successful Madness got, the more the management felt we needed a more professional road crew and this attitude contributed to Chalky and Toks' eventual exit. I should have stuck up for them more and I regret that I didn't. In the end they were issued warnings, but before they were pushed they walked. They didn't want to give the management the satisfaction of firing them.

Toks: I've heard that Chalky and me were given warnings, but I don't remember getting any. Kellogg's* was involved with the band when all of that happened. I could actually see his point of view: he was just a stooge for Stiff Records, who felt that they needed other people working with Madness. Chalky and me could only do so much, but it's fair to say we weren't technically gifted. I think there were times when Kellogg's tried his best to get us sacked. He would do things to try and wind us up, hoping that one of us would thump him, but I just used to laugh at him.

Chalky and me did walk away. We left, but we never held any grudges. For my part it was because I had a load of mates going off to live in kibbutzes in the Middle East and I went too. I know Lee feels that he didn't stick up for us, but it wasn't really needed. He is a very sweet man and I love him like a brother – a lot of people feel this way about him. Lee actually gave Chalky and me a credit on the 7 album.

While I was travelling the band sent me a letter telling me they were going to release a version of Labi Siffre's 'It Must Be Love'. I wrote back saying, 'Fuck me, I've only been gone three months and you've all turned into hippies!' It went on to be one of their biggest hits. Not long after I got back from Israel, I somehow got roped

* Stiff Records tour/company liaison manager John Kalinowski.

253

into going out to Japan with Madness. We all stayed mates.*

Nineteen seventy-nine had been an amazing year for me. Madness were on the up. We had our first record deal, with a label that I respected. I was making new friends among bands like The Specials and, most of, The Selecter. Madness had our first record released and we'd been on *Top Of The Pops*, the best and biggest music show around – where I'd seen Alice Cooper, Bowie and Bolan perform when I was a teenager.

I was also having a lot of fun being on tour and discovering new places, meeting lots of new people and having loads of new experiences. But, as wonderful as 1979 was, there was no way that I could imagine how amazing the next few years were to be. We'd release loads more records, have several hits and a number one with 'House Of Fun'. I'd also travel to places I could only previously have read about in *National Geographic* or *Hello* magazine.

But when you're caught up in all of what's happening, tomorrow's just another day.

To be continued... maybe!

---

* The important thing is that Chalky, Toks and me have remained friends. I last saw Toks when he showed up at a Tunes in the Dunes festival in Cornwall. I'd been in a pub before the concert and as I looked out across the road I spotted him. It took him a moment to notice me and then he strolled over.

"Thommo, how long have you been here then?" he asked. I replied, "About an hour," then we set about having a drink and a laugh. He didn't have a ticket for the gig so I told him, "No problem." All he needed to do was hold my saxophone and say he was my sax roadie. With a grin on his face, he legged it off back down the road with my sax under his arm.

AFTERWORD
Davey Payne

"Did you see Davey Payne smashing up his sax?" This was a conversation I overheard from a toilet cubicle at a Kilburn and the High Roads gig at Hornsey College of Art. Little did I know that these guys would go on to become one of the most loved bands in the country. Sometimes searching for an original solo can take you to the edge. Lee's music is from the soul; his life and experience, you either feel it or you don't. Lee and I have to go down a different road, gut-felt originality. Lee also understands the theatre, humour and drama in music: sadness, memories, happy moments, family and friends are expressed through his sax, communicating with the audience and creating a synergy with the band, not just a string of clichéd notes.

I first met Lee in person at a Blockheads gig at Hammersmith Odeon, after sound checking. He gave me a copy of their single 'The Prince' on 2Tone Records which I still have today.

EARLY DISCOGRAPHY – 1979
(compiled by Tony Murphy)

ALBUMS IN UPPER CASE / singles in lower

The Prince (Thompson)
B-side: Madness (Prince Buster)
A-side inspired by ska artist Prince Buster – composer of
B-side
Released 01/09/79
UK Chart Peak: 16
Recorded at Pathway Studios
Produced by Clive Langer and Alan Winstanley

ONE STEP BEYOND...
1.　One Step Beyond... (Prince Buster)
2.　My Girl (Barson)
3.　Night Boat To Cairo (McPherson/Barson)
4.　Believe Me (Barson/Hasler)
5.　Land Of Hope And Glory (Foreman/Thompson)
6.　The Prince

7.   Tarzan's Nuts (Sydney Lee – arranged Smyth/Barson)

8.   In The Middle Of The Night (McPherson/Foreman)

9.   Bed And Breakfast Man (Barson)

10. Razor Blade Alley (Thompson)

11. Swan Lake (Tchaikovsky – arranged Barson)

12. Rockin' In A♭ (Willy Wurlitzer)

13. Mummy's Boy (Bedford)

14. Madness

15. Chipmunks Are Go! (C. Smyth/B. Smyth)

Released 19/10/79

UK Album Chart Peak: 2

Recorded at Eden Studios

Produced by Clive Langer and Alan Winstanley

One Step Beyond…

Seven-inch B-side: Mistakes (Hasler/Barson)

Twelve-inch B-side: Mistakes/Nutty Theme (McPherson/ Thompson)

Released 10/11/79

UK Chart Peak: 7

Recorded at Eden Studios

Produced by Clive Langer and Alan Winstanley

GIGS AND ACTIVITIES
(all gigs based in London prior to July 1979)

1978

April 5	Nightingale Pub, Crouch End (Invaders)
April 22	Gavin Rodgers' house (Invaders)
July 3	William Ellis School (Invaders – without Suggs, who attends)
No date:	3 C's Club (Invaders – without Suggs, who attends)
November 10	Acklam Hall (Invaders – with Suggs)

1979

January 1	London Film Makers Co-op, Camden (Invaders)
January 7	Nashville Rooms, Kensington (Invaders)
January 16	Dublin Castle, Camden (Invaders)
January 22	Music Machine, Camden (Morris and the Minors)

May 3	Hope & Anchor, Islington (Madness)
May 4	Nashville Rooms
May 7	Windsor Castle, Harrow Road
May 19	Mentioned by The Specials in *Melody Maker*

June 1	Dublin Castle
June 8	Nashville Rooms/Dublin Castle Supported The Specials at Nashville before playing DC
June 15	Dublin Castle
June 16	Pathway Studios – demo recordings of 'The Prince' and 'My Girl' produced by Clive Langer
June 24	Hope & Anchor
June 28	Nashville Rooms
June 29	Dublin Castle

July 6	Dublin Castle
July 8	Hope & Anchor
July 14	Eric's, Liverpool, with The Specials
July 21	Electric Ballroom, Camden, supporting The Specials
July 29	Lyceum Ballroom, Strand, supporting The Pretenders
July 31	Pied Bull, Angel

August 10	'The Prince' released on 2Tone Records, charts at 16
August 14	John Peel session recorded for Radio 1
August 15	Rock Garden, Covent Garden

August 17	Stiff Records party/Dave Robinson's wedding at Clarendon Ballroom, Hammersmith
August 18	*NME* feature on Madness
August 20	Hope & Anchor
August 21	Hope & Anchor
August 22	Madness meet Dave Robinson at Stiff Records
August 24	Eric's, Liverpool
August 25	Witcombe Lodge, Cheltenham, supporting Pam Nestor
August 26	Lyceum Ballroom
August 27	John Peel session broadcast, featuring 'The Prince', 'Bed And Breakfast Man', 'Land Of Hope And Glory' and 'Stepping Into Line'
August 31	Nashville Rooms SOLD OUT
September 1	The Factory, Manchester
September 3	Madness sign to Stiff Records
September 5	*Top Of The Pops* recording/Dingwalls, Camden
September 6	*Top Of The Pops* broadcast
September 8	Friars Aylesbury supporting Secret Affair
September 9	Nashville Rooms
September 11	Eden Studios, Acton
	Recording begins on *One Step Beyond...* album, produced by Clive Langer and Alan Winstanley
September 19	Second *Top Of The Pops* appearance
September 20	Second *Top Of The Pops* broadcast

October 2	Warwick Hall, Coventry
October 4	F Club, Leeds
October 5	Porterhouse Club, Retford
October 6	Huddersfield Polytechnic
October 7	Hope & Anchor
October 8	Civic Hall, Oldham
October 9	University of Nottingham
October 12	Electric Ballroom supported by Bad Manners / Echo and the Bunnymen
October 13	Brighton Polytechnic
October 19	*One Step Beyond...* album released, charts at 2
October 26	'One Step Beyond...' single released, charts at 7

2TONE TOUR *(with The Specials/The Selecter)*

October 16	Rehearsals at The Roundhouse, Chalk Farm
October 19	Top Rank, Brighton
October 20	Oasis, Swindon
October 21	Stateside Centre, Bournemouth
October 22	University of Exeter
October 23	Fiesta, Plymouth
October 26	University of East Anglia, Norwich
October 27	Hatfield Polytechnic
	During The Selecter's set, violence erupts. Thugs claiming to be members of the Anti-Nazi League break in and attack some audience members, claiming they are National Front supporters. Ten people are hospitalised, eleven are arrested.

October 28	Civic Hall, Wolverhampton
October 29	Top Rank, Birmingham
October 31	Victoria Hall, Hanley
November 1	Golden Palms, Blackburn
November 2	Preston Polytechnic
November 4	Top Rank, Sheffield
November 5	De Montfort Hall, Leicester
November 6	Guildhall, Portsmouth
November 7	*Top Of The Pops*/Top Rank, Cardiff Madness charter a small plane to fly to Cardiff for their set
November 9	Mayfair, Newcastle
November 10	University of Stirling
November 11	Glasgow
November 12	Tiffany's, Edinburgh
November 13	Ruffles, Aberdeen
November 14	Ayr Pavilion

END OF 2TONE TOUR

November 16	Electric Ballroom
November 17	Electric Ballroom

<u>*USA TOUR*</u>

November 22	Mudd Club, New York
November 23	Hurrah, New York
November 24	Paradise Club, Boston
November 25	Tier 3, New York
November 26	Hot Club, Philadelphia
November 29	The Whisky A Go Go, Los Angeles
November 30	The Mabuhay, San Francisco

December 11   *The Old Grey Whistle Test*, performing 'Night Boat To Cairo' and 'Bed And Breakfast Man'

UK HEADLINE TOUR supported by The VIPs

December 12   Top Rank, Brighton
December 13   Hemel Hempstead Pavilion
December 14   Odeon, Canterbury
December 15   Bracknell Sports Centre
December 16   Stateside Centre, Bournemouth
December 17   Pier Pavilion, Hastings
December 18   *Multi-Coloured Swap Shop* TV show
December 19   Interview for Radio Luxembourg
December 20   Victoria Hall, Hanley
December 21   King's Hall, Derby
                     'My Girl' released, charts at 3
December 22   De Montfort Hall, Leicester
December 23   Locarno, Bristol
December 24   'My Girl' video shoot at Dublin Castle
December 29   Friars Aylesbury
December 30   Lyceum Ballroom

LEE'S SONGS
(as writer or co-writer)

The Prince: After reading about this band from the Midlands playing the same genre of music that we were into, Suggs and Barzo decided to go and along and investigate The Specials live. Jerry Dammers was invited back to Suggs' abode, whereupon they talked music throughout the night. By the end of this chat, Jerry had offered Madness, via Suggs, a one-off single release on the 2Tone label. We had a few self-penned tunes – 'Memories', 'Mistakes', 'Nutty Theme', 'My Girl' – but none suiting the label's style. I sat down in my Caledonian Road flat and listened to some Prince Buster tunes from his fab greatest hits album, using the words from some of the lyrics. A friend (Tracey Barnett) asked me what I was doing playing the same tracks over and over. I told her I was writing a tribute to the Jamaican artist for a possible single release.

Razor Blade Alley: I had a sleazy, jazzy idea I wanted to use for this tune about a young lad catching a dose from a night of unprotected casual sex – not through personal experience, mind you. I'd recently seen a film called *The Boys In Company C*: an American soldier visits a whorehouse and leaves with an unwanted disease in his sack. (Also, the other inspiration for the lyric was from a movie called *The Last Detail* with Jack Nicholson.) I had the bassline and melody in my head but was unable to put this across to the band. So I hummed it to Mike to sprinkle his magic on the song and *voila!* I felt like a knight without my shining armour on.

Land Of Hope And Glory: A quirky number Chrissy Boy put together, a very uncommercial tune all about my experience at approved school in the early 70s, based in Ramsey, near Harwich. I was just fourteen and taken away by the authorities when I'd become a thorn in the side of many of the community where I lived, as well as the surrounding areas. I was basically a little fucker and the courts had had enough of my mate Bob Townshend and me. It was painful, especially at that age, but it was necessary and set me straight. A bit of discipline never hurt anybody. I'd highly recommend it. I'm a believer in conscription – taught me how to make my bed.

Embarrassment: Again, I used the melody from a Prince Buster tune, 'Free Love', for the lyric. I then passed this to Mike as the pressure was on to get that difficult second album completed. The lyric was actually finished as it was being recorded. Mike had come up with a Motown feel and I was really over the moon with everyone's input. It ticked every box and I felt this was a turning point (after the brilliant 'Baggy Trousers'). 'Embarrassment' is the story of my mixed-race niece, the whispers and lies, bigotry and cloak-and-dagger shyte, that was going around at the time of her birth.

Close Escape: On our debut album Suggs had written a lyric that totally appealed to me: in the middle of the night a knicker fetishist would go creeping for frilly lingerie. A true story apparently. It had that warped sense of this poor fellow with issues and tissues. He's not harming anyone but himself so it's bittersweet, disturbing but also comedic. I kept him around for the second album, now moving on to making obscene phone calls from ye olde public telephone kiosks, fingering through the pages, half-ejaculating at the thought – a nuisance to say the least. You'd get murdered for it today. We should bring him into the new millennium maybe?

On The Beat Pete: The joys of being a bobby on the street, eh? At the time of writing this an adult and two kids had been charged with the murder of a policeman after a bungled burglary, by dragging him 100 yards down the road under their vehicle – the ripple effect of tragedy is never ending! I put a Norman-Wisdom-meets-Inspector-Clouseau angle on this, the happy-go-lucky copper in an ideal world, meeting the people in his community, giving them that personal touch: "How are things? You looking after yourself? Don't do anything I wouldn't do." A bobby who is not a soft touch but cares about what goes on in his manor, on his watch, a Dixon of Dock Green dreaming on...

Overdone: Mums, eh? You can't live with them or without them. I caused her so much grief in my youth. Then I left home, picked up a saxophone and taught myself to play it. Okay, it was a loud cacophony of honks, blurps and squeaks initially, but as time passed I made her proud and I was able to purchase Mum and Dad their own house in Great Yarmouth. Then I made sure she was looked after when Dad passed. The sax on this track was ad libbed straight from the heart. I just blew what I felt – same as for 'Embarrassment' solo.

Tomorrow's Dream: I'd been reading up on animal experimentation, watching 1950s and 60s footage of torture of our furry friends. All in the name of scientific progress, pushing the boudaries of medicine and modern science, etc. It's a very dark subject and I put myself in that cage. Ronald Reagan's Star Wars programme was also in full swing, with laser beams supposed to be able to take out whole towns and cities from the other side of the world – and the Vietnam war still raw from only a decade earlier. No change there really!

Pac-A-Mac: Back to that 'shining armour' subject again: a nonsensical, safe sex-related lyric about… well, safe sex. The many diseases that can be transmitted by unprotected sex in the heat of the moment. Ouch!

Promises Promises: All the pledges made when you plan to wed your loved one, until death do you part, and sign on the dotted line. Sometimes it works. An old pal of mine was married for over twenty years, then decided to lock her in

267

the house, eventually stabbing her. She got out of Dodge sharpish and he got a seven stretch. This was also based on the promises made by Thatcher's Tory government: although some of her ideas were promising, she stupidly broke the camel's back by bringing in that ridiculous poll-tax crap.

Benny Bullfrog: Whilst recording the 7 album back in Antigua in July 1981, I was looking for some inspiration on the white sandy beach. The royal wedding and the pressures of stepping into that arena had crossed my mind. George (who had debuted on *One Step Beyond...*, appearing again on *Absolutely*) was a focus, but he'd already been sniffing knickers and jerking down the blower. Then, as if by magic, a fluorescent green, slimy frog with pillar-box-red eyeballs slapped itself onto my bedroom window. I put pen to paper and by the end of the evening I'd completed the lyric, ha, ha! Found a fiver.

When Dawn Arrives: Rent boys and male prostitution. Don't ask me where that came out of – certainly not through personal experience. Dave Robbo at Stiff suggested we go out to Compass Point, Nassau, in the Caribbean to broaden our horizons. What did we return with? An album that could have been recorded in Hackney. Overall, it's rather dark, when I think of the paradise we were in.

Blue Skinned Beast: This is my take on the Falklands war and the media coverage at the time. Unbelievable. One tabloid decided to print on the front page that they would be sending out crates of beer for our boys in the Falkland

Islands. 'Blue-skinned beast' was my image of Thatcher at the time; government ratings are starting to wane so let's create a diversion and pick a fight with the Argentinians. Though they did attempt to take the Falklands, England took its eye off the ball and was found asleep on the job. Military cutbacks was the issue. Still, the Tories secured another term in office.

Calling Cards: A day in the life of a gang of fraudsters based on the Old Kent Road. They would collect their credit cards from various meeting points and spend the day picking up various items from shops and retail stores, from Rolex watches and prestige cars to the latest electrical appliances and the latest on offer the technology field. They played banks around the world in a game of cat and mouse on a grand scale.

Are You Coming (With Me): I used to hang around with a friend that I knew was a heroin addict. I was trying to get him away from the company he'd been drawn into. It worked out positively and he's turned it round.

House Of Fun: The coming of age theme, all the joy, fun and adventures awaiting you when you reach sixteen. And the flipside of the coin? My granddaughter was sixteen this year. We've decided to move the celebrations to March 2021!

March Of The Gherkins: You know that fleshy thing that dangles from the back of your throat? The thing that vibrates when you laugh out loud, when you show the world your fillings and your sides ache from the absolute joy of the company you're with and want to be with. Not losing sight of that, if you can't be with the one you love, love the one you're with. (Have I heard that somewhere before?)

Brand New Beat: The Thatcher government got me all anxious about the direction we were going in, i.e. totalitarianism with police powers to stop and search, the Special Patrol Group who would drive about in fifteen-seater vans, pulling you up for no particular reason (other than maybe being black). I got pulled up whilst bread and dripping. I was totally freaked out, the democratic system was being threatened. A New World Order theme, rather relevant in the present climate.

Time For Tea: I'd read about a kid buying some glue from a hardware shop. After inhaling the solvent, he climbed into this hideaway for some solitude. Unfortunately, it was a dumped fridge on some wasteland.

Give Me A Reason: Here I put myself into the mind of a bullying stepfather, blaming the reason for his actions on his past upbringing.

I'll Compete: Chasing the carrot on the giant record deck that is the industry. Being disillusioned and lost in a museum of has-beens, not enjoying the position you're in but contractually obliged to fulfil. Thankfully, we were put down.

Uncle Sam: The UK's obligations to America, how we were becoming more influenced by consumerism and how I was unwittingly being sucked in by it all. The UK's identity, I felt, was being stripped away and I was holding the steamer and scraper. The Greenham Common women were putting up one hell of a fight, but we all knew what the end result would be. A theme with crude satire injected throughout.

I Pronounce You: A marriage arranged overseas to a future husband, chosen for you, who you've never even met.

Beat The Bride: You always hurt the one(s) you love. When times get tough financially, don't take it out on the people nearest and dearest to you. Rise above it. Go hire a tank (preferably hybrid LPG) and rob a bank.

Love Struck: Getting rat-faced at a party, losing everything in your possession, all your friends and family giving up on you, finding yourself collapsed face-down in a pool of nastiness, comatose in a park somewhere around the London N15 area.

Drip Fed Fred: A little story of cops, robbers, low-lifers and hero Freddie. The public demands Fredrick be released back into the community on the grounds of being well behaved and he thereby runs for office. But his life is sadly cut short by a nonce inmate who cuts off his fuel line. An idea based on my dad and sung by another hero, the late, great Mr Ian Dury.

Elysium: The thickness of a person's skin can often be gauged by the content of their heart and soul. Once you understand what's been planted in their heads you can peel back the body make-up, their armour.

ACKNOWLEDGEMENTS

My heartfelt thanks to my friends, family and colleagues for taking the time to share their memories and recollections of our activities. And thank you to Ian Snowball for all of his help writing this book.